AFRICAN WRITERS SERIES   FOUNDING EDITOR   Chinua Achebe

Ayi Kwei Armah

Fragments

HEINEMANN
LONDON · IBADAN · NAIROBI

Heinemann Educational Books Ltd
22 Bedford Square, London WC1B 3HH
P.M.B. 5205, Ibadan · P.O. Box 45314, Nairobi
Heinemann Educational Books Inc.
70 Court Street, Portsmouth, New Hampshire 03801, USA
EDINBURGH MELBOURNE AUCKLAND
SINGAPORE KUALA LUMPUR NEW DELHI
KINGSTON

ISBN 0 435 90154 0

© Ayi Kwei Armah 1969
First published by Houghton Mifflin Co. 1970
First published by Heinemann 1974
First published in African Writers Series 1974
Reprinted 1979
Reset 1983
Reprinted 1985, 1987

*This edition has now been
completely reset and page numbers
do not now correspond with
earlier editions*

Printed and bound in Great Britain by
Richard Clay Ltd, Bungay, Suffolk

for AMA ATA
& ANA LIVIA

By the same author

The Beautyful Ones Are Not Yet Born
Why Are We So Blest?
The Healers

1 : Naana

EACH THING that goes away returns and nothing in the end is lost.
The great friend throws all things apart and brings all things
together again. That is the way everything goes and turns round.
That is how all living things come back after long absences, and in
the whole great world all things are living things. All that goes
returns. He will return.

How can I not know it when all my years I have watched the sun go
down times unending toward the night only to come again from the
dawn the opposite way? Too true, it is so long since last I saw the
sun, going or coming. But my skin continues still to tell the heat
from the cold, and I know it is I who have changed, not the changing
circle of the world itself. And yet even here things have come about
lately to put into me more fearful doubts than my tired soul can hold.
Have two nights passed? Or is it two whole weeks that have passed
me by?

I had moved myself into the middle of the yard, and sitting by the
stairs where they begin I had spent forgetful time bathing in warmth
of such surpassing sweetness that I was sure I was beginning even
now to see the sun again. And then they came and broke my peace,
saying I had been sitting out there in the cold for hours. Surprised
and angry that they were moving me another time, I was sharpening
words to tell them I had only come to take in this heat of the sun, till
one of them, was it Efua? said in her gentle voice words that touched
my soul with fear.

Night fell long ago, Naana.

I was amazed. I was going to tell her she was wrong, that I had
surely felt the sun touch my skin and leave its warmth on it, but then

I thought again and thinking made me hold my peace.

I am a person no more, unable to help myself. What is still left of my bones and of the flesh that clings to it would make a small enough burden for any head, but for *them* it has too long been an annoying burden. I am old and of no use to anyone, but I am a mouth that continues to eat pepper and taste salt. I am such a mouth, joined to an end that runs with waste, spending others' love that has long since disappeared. Is that not enough? Or should I go and add to this a spray of words against the angry face of everyone? Only the strong ones can fail to be understood and still survive, and I am of no use to anyone. If I should see a thing which all around me think they do not see, why will I in my foolishness shout against all the strength of their unseeing eyes? The witches saw things denied to others; beyond that they talked of what it was they had seen, and were destroyed. It is a long time since I heard of any witch thrown out of her secrecy, but souls are broken all the same. If I see things unseen by those who have eyes, why should my wisest speech not be silence?

One thing I will continue to tell them over and over again: he will return. They who have their eyes with them still but are nonetheless the shadowy ones, they will not have the hardness to destroy me for knowing that, because it is a knowledge close to their souls also, though they know it only as a wish, and it is almost a stranger to them. Their wishes are the closest thing they have to the beauty of long peaceful dreams, and in their wishing they too want this return. The things they want it for, the wishes below – those are other things to load my soul with fear.

There have been some dreams abroad, and I am afraid. There should be dreams before returns, as before goings, before everything. That is only just. But these have been woven of such heavy earth that they will load his spirit down and after they have touched him it will never fly again.

Two such dreams I have heard from the mouth of Efua herself. Oh great friend, a human mother should not have such dreams against the coming of her own flesh and her loved one's soul. Even cats have learned to turn the hunger for the newly born against their own entrails.

Perhaps in years alone Baako himself is a child no more. But what is a traveler just returned from far journeys started years ago if not a new one all again?

And Araba too. I have heard of the dreams she has had to welcome her returning brother. Yet who am I to throw sour words against the dreams of the eager sister and the eager mother? I too have had my dreams of his return, and they too have been filled with things to give rest to tired flesh heavy things, things of heavy earth. I have also dreamed of riches and greatness for Baako, and they were not for him alone. I have known that if riches and greatness should ever cross his path and walk with him to the end of his days, and if in this slippery place he shoud one day find firm standing for his tired young soles, I am not one he will choose to forget.

Everyone who goes returns. He will come. He will be changed, but we shall welcome him as the same. That is the circle. There has been a lot of cruelty done, but nothing has been done so grave that in this case the circle should be broken. Nothing was left out before he was taken up into the sky to cross the sea and to go past the untouchable horizon itself. I watched everything that night, and I am weak, but with the little strength that I still had in me I would myself have stopped the drunken Foli if he had gone wrong anywhere, adding things unknown to those gone before, or leaving out any of the words and actions they have left us to guide us on the circular way. Nothing at all was left out. The uncle called upon the nephew the protection of the old ones gone before. The circle was not broken. The departed one will return.

His uncle Foli has always been one to have a spirit flawed by the heaviness of flesh too often listened to. But that night his words had a perfect completeness that surprised me and told me the departed ones are still watching over those they left here above. Even Foli felt their presence. His soul within those hours left the heavy body so as to be with the departed ones, to ask their help upon the head of the one about to go. Nothing was said then that was not to be said, and nothing remained unsaid for which there was a need.

Where you are going,
go softly.

Nananom,
you who have gone before,
see that his body does not lead him
into snares made for the death of spirits.
You who are going now,
do not let your mind become persuaded
that you walk alone.
There are no humans born alone.
You are a piece of us,
of those gone before
and who will come again.
A piece of us, go
and come a piece of us.
You will not be coming,
when you come,
the way you went away.
You will come stronger,
to make us stronger,
wiser,
to guide us with your wisdom.
Gain much from this going.
Gain the wisdom
to turn your back on the wisdom
of Ananse.
Do not be persuaded you will fill your stomach faster
if you do not have others' to fill.
There are no humans who walk this earth alone.

But that there was such hot desire impatient at his departure for his return, that I did not see. So much else around me drew my spirit into that night. And the words took me away into a past that filled me with satisfaction because everything in it was full of understanding. After the words, there were sounds that rose before me as if all this crowded present had never come at all, and days and years already gone had come again to live with us, their sounds bringing clearness out of dim forgotten nights. Not even Foli's voice, used so often for deceit, could scrape the peace and understanding of those ancient words.

A human being alone
is a thing more sad than any lost animal

and nothing destroys the soul
like its aloneness.

Only after those words did Foli think to begin pouring out the schnapps he had been holding in those hands of his which hate so much to let hot drink escape. He had kept the spirits waiting like begging children for the drink of their own libation and, thirsty drunkard that he has always been, even when at last he began to pour it out he only let go of little miserly drops, far from enough to end the long thirst of a single one of those gone before. I could see his eyes, with a lot of the drunken white showing underneath, and the black of them stuck almost to their upper lids. Slyly like a thief he was measuring the bottle in his soul. The less he poured out to end the thirst of the ghosts the more the bottom would hold for his own dry mouth. And yet this man with his shriveled soul found all the words to speed Baako into alien worlds and to protect him there. Perfect words, with nothing missing and nothing added that should not have been there. It was dark, but the light from behind us came to us in the doorway and caught the miserly drink as it fell, making each drop disappear a shiny bead.

The unbelievable thing was that outside there was movement in all this stillness. Lights came casting giant leaf shadows upon the walls inside from cars returning, lights that moved up and down and across before dying with the passing of the cars. They reminded me then of the moving shadows and lights I had seen many years and nights ago, when the cinema lorry used to come. One car even blew its horn, the blower not knowing that so close to him there were humans talking to the spirits gone before, even if there was only the drunkard Foli to speak in the name of those yet to go.

Always
there has been a danger in such departures.
Much of our blood has run to waste
yet we will not speak of ways
to stop the coming and the going
for we are not mad with the sorrow of moments that pass.
Always
the danger of death,
the death of the body,
death of the soul

alone on seas that know no ending,
hanging in the endless sky
alone beyond all horizons
where our highest hills are themselves too small,
alone in the opposite lands,
lands of the ghosts,
alone in white men's lands.

There are dangers in this life
but fathers,
do not fill your grandson here with fears.
The danger of death we have with us
around us everywhere at home.
It is the promise of those gone before.
Let him hear that.
Let him not forget its truth
and give him courage to understand it.
Watch over him, fathers.
Watch over him
and let him prosper
there where he is going.
And when he returns
let his return, like rain,
bring us your blessings and fruits,
your blessings
your help
in this life you have left us to fight alone.
With your wisdom
let him go,
let him come.
And you, traveler about to go,
Go and return,
Go, come.

Even coming from a man himself so blemished, they were perfect words. I looked at Baako. He had the smile of the young on his face. For him all this was something from another place, and he was impatient like a child to see it end. He would spend the night hanging in the sky, he had told me that before, and already his eyes were filled with an eagerness to go.

The pig Foli, in spite of the beauty of the words he had spoken, remained inside his soul a lying pig. A shameful lot more than a whole half bottle of the drink had remained unpoured, and now he went and took from among his many shiny things a glass to pour the traveler's drink of ceremony for Baako. It was a very small glass he took, the shriveled soul, the better to keep what remained of the drink for his own parched throat. It makes me weaker still, to think how many times the softness and the greed of our bodies makes us wish we could continue to cheat those who have gone before and even those coming after us. And then what was most amazing, the glass itself was not a hollow glass at all, but a special thing made to deceive the seeing eye, with a bottom thick and solid almost halfway to the top, so that only a very shallow bowl, almost flat, was left to hold the drink. Into this Foli poured the schnapps for his own nephew Baako. All the time his eyes were sharpened to see that not one more drop escaped to give peace to the unsatisfied tongues of the ancestors he had already cheated. His filthy ears must have heard something from the spirits even then, because with no one having mentioned his drunken gluttony he sought to give saving reasons for himself, saying,

"We must not make him drunk. He is young, and he will be travelling in the night."

As for Baako himself it seemed even the little he was given was too much for his tongue. I saw tears in his eyes a moment after he put that amazing glass to his lips, and afterward he seemed glad there had been no more of the spirit in it for him to drink. I looked from the young man to his uncle, and then my blood was poisoned with the fear of what would happen if Foli's greed for drink was allowed to break the circle and to spoil all the perfect beauty of the libation. And Foli, he had turned his back with the rolls of skin on it, and he was preparing to take himself a glass with no false cheating bottom and to pour his blind soul a full drink of the spirit. There was nothing other for me to do. I waited till he had drawn the glass. It was a big one. Then I said,

"It is your mind to pour me out a drink in that, Foli."

Over his face there came that anger which shame so swiftly changes to a generous smile.

"But Naana, is it good for you also to drink?"

"We give our ghosts to drink, or am I a liar? And what is an old woman but the pregnancy that will make another ghost?"

"It is so strong, you know, schnapps."

"Yes, Foli. And is it you now telling me the weak ones have no need of what is strong?"

"Ahh, Naana." He sighed, but there was nothing he could do. He looked at the bottle in his hand, and I could see his stomach sink with thinking how the drink was going down. Then he smiled and held out the glass to me. I took it. With a very white smile he began to pour, fearfully and slowly, like a man forced to shed the blood of his own grandmother, and he was telling me,

"I will leave it up to you to tell me when to stop."

I did not let him use my own shame against me. I looked into his face and I also smiled a false smile to answer his, and continued to hold his eyes with mine as he poured the drink.

"Tell me when to stop," he said again. The glass was only half full, the python.

I smiled, and looked at him. His pouring hand was now beginning to shake, but I let him pour until the glass was full, and even then I said nothing. He stopped himself. He was frowning now, not knowing what to say.

"Naana," he was beginning. I could hear him, but only like a voice from very far away. "Naana, are you going to drink all that yourself?"

Quietly I went past him into the doorway where he had stood offering libation to those gone before, and in the same place where he had let fall those miserly drops I poured down everything in the glass, and it was only after that that I opened my mouth again:

"Nananom, drink to your thirst, and go with the young one. Protect him well, and bring him back, to us, to you."

As I came back into the room Foli met me with words,

"But I poured . . ."

"It was not enough," I answered him. "I am not quarreling with you: it was enough. You learned so well the words you spoke to the dead ones this night. Did no one also teach you the power of the anger of the departed? How did you forget, then? Or was the present growling of your belly a greater thing than Baako's going and the whole stream of his life after that? The spirits would have been angry, and they would have turned their anger against him. He would have been destroyed."

From speaking alone a tiredness came over me then as if many hands had beaten me each one gently but all together for long days on end. I fell on a soft long seat opposite the one Baako was sitting on, quietly watching what he could not yet have understood, and I slept because when I woke up there were many people and a terrible hurry all around me and a mad blowing of many horns from people's cars outside.

"Naana, you will come in may car. That is where Baako will be," Foli said. I had indeed asked to go the last miles with the departing one. There had been many things in me for him, but they were not things I could say, and so sitting close to him would be good. I was happy Foli had remembered, but I had not known it would be in his car, with him so full of drink already. But, as if he had caught my waking thoughts, he said quietly, so that I was ashamed,

"I will not be the one driving, Naana. The driver is here. It will not be long before we go."

The horns and the shouting stopped outside. Inside there was the sound of songs from another of Foli's shiny things. For a long time I listened and was lost, till I heard Foli shout to Baako and another friend, as if I were not there,

"Look at your grandmother, listening as if she can understand."

Before I could become angry I saw it was true. I had not understood a single word, and yet this was something I had not known before Foli spoke. Listening to the sounds, I had thought I knew what the words were saying also.

"Who are they?" I asked.

"Who?"

"The people singing. Those playing,"

"Ah. Afro-Americans."

"Americans?"

"Yes," Foli said.

"It was as if I understood what they were saying."

Several people laughed and I felt like a child, not knowing what I had done to make them laugh like that.

"Their people were Africans." It was Baako who said this. Afraid to raise more laughter against myself, I shook my head with the perfect understanding that was not in it. I had not understood the words at all, but the sounds, above all the cries of the man who sang most of the beginnings, and the women's voices, many, many women's voices always there around him to catch his pain and make it into something almost sweet, that was all familiar to me somewhere. And also beneath it all the thing that went on always and would not let me escape, heavy like a sound of doom, that also I knew.

The sounds were cut off suddenly in the middle of a long shout because everybody said it was time to go, but the sadness remained with me.

That night I saw more things to astonish me in this place and to make me feel how much I have become a stranger here, because these are things whose meaning I will never understand before the time of my going comes. In my mind also I walked across strange lands where I had never been before.

Sometimes I know my blindness was sent to me to save me from the madness that would surely have come with seeing so much that was not te be understood. Going with Baako to see him go, we went out of Foli's room and the many cars drove into the night, but soon there was no longer any night to see. Where the cars were passing, in the open streets themselves, not even in people's homes, there were lights so many and so strong that even I saw then the gap of a young breadseller's teeth, as if the night had never come – and she was not near, but safe beyond the road, on the gutter's other side. And yet no one thought to say anything: not Foli, and of the young ones none at all. So I kept my peace but whenever I saw Baako's face in the corner I asked inside myself if it was possible that all of them were growing to be men thinking this was the world, and this the night.

I closed my eyes against the night that had disappeared outside, and I saw Baako roaming in unknown, forbidden places, just born there again after a departure and a death somewhere. He had arrived from beneath the horizon and standing in a large place that was open and filled with many winds, he was lonely. But suddenly he was not alone, but walking one among many people. All the people were white people all knowing only how to speak the white people's languages. Always, after saying anything, however small or large, they shook their white heads solemnly, as if they were the ones gone before. Some touched hands, slowly. But Baako walked among them neither touched nor seen, like a ghost in an overturned world in which all human flesh was white. And some of these people bore in their arms things of a beauty so great that I thought then in my soul this was the way the spirit land must be. Only it was a beauty that frightened also, and before I could remember again that he was not yet gone I had made in my fear a hurried asking for protection on Baako's head.

We did not go with him inside the airplane to see him go. We were not allowed to go with him, but parted company in a room large as Nyankom, Esuano and Patase all put together, and in this place also we had the amazing brightness all around us.

Then we went outside to a long white fence behind which we stood with others like us who had come to weep for a departing one, and after a long time we saw the line of people, many white people but also others who were black, go like gentle ghosts into the airplane. When it swallowed Baako in his turn, I could look no more. I did not turn to see it as it began to go into the air, though Foli was by me telling me to look, because like a child he saw only beauty in the going of the thing. The heavy sound made me fear for Baako. But I remembered how perfect the words had been for his departure and his protection, and I was happy inside myself that I had taken the drink from Foli and given the ancestors their need. The circle was not broken in any place.

They will protect him. How can it then be said that he will not come?

2 : Edin

IT WAS NOT just in the mind, this need for flight. It was also in the body, possessingly physical, a need she had begun to feel with an intensity that increased steadily with the passage of this time, a need after a morning's work at the hospital, to go, just go as far out as she could and leave behind her the clinic buildings with their modern façades that were the only modern things about them, to leave the rows of barracks with their green windows, the only things the nurses had for quarters, to leave the whole aborted town just to get out and keep going in the attempt, however doomed, to forget that now the sum of her life was only that she was here in another defeated and defeating place, to forget all the reminders of futility.

As she came out and closed the consultation room door behind her, the duty nurse got up from her chair and came over to her, touching her starched white and green cap in a gesture that could have been taken for a salute had it not been so feminine. The nurse came forward with a certain languorous swing to her walk. She was smiling, showing the beauty of her white, even teeth, but there was also a genuine inward joy.

"I'll be coming back late this afternoon," Juana said. "Take only a few people on the waiting list. No one earlier than three-thirty."

"Yes, Doctor," the nurse said. Her right hand had descended to the lapel of her green uniform, picking at something invisible, and she was still smiling as Juana took her keys out of her left pocket and walked down the length of the corridor and out into the sun, to the parking lot.

"You saw a lot of patients this morning, Doctor."

"Yes, Patience. And you, you must be tired too."

"We here are more used to it, all this."

Juana sensed the unavoidable estrangement, the politeness of distances created for strangers like herelf, no matter how close they tried to come, and she was glad the nurse did not continue. She had not been aware the other was following her. In the shade of the trees where she had parked the car mango leaves had fallen onto the hood and one which had not lost its greenness had also dropped and gotten caught between the windshield and the left wiper. As she removed the leaf she turned to the nurse and asked her: "Do you need a ride some place?"

"Yes, please, Doctor."

There was a time, in the beginning, when she had tried to melt all this formality by having the nurses drop the title and call her by her name. But she had only succeeded in embarrassing them, and in many wordless, polite ways they had made her understand that it was strange and threatening to them, this need of hers to have them desert a familiar reality in which there was the respected Doctor and Senior Nurses and Senior Assistant Nurses and Junior Nurses and little Nurses in Training, and the titles meant a world into which they had struggled and were still struggling to fit their own lives. With the coming of this understanding she had given up, though often she still found herself needing to reassure herself that some day the deadly seriousness people here invested in these external things, from the titles to the dozens of graded types of uniform, would crack and let some kind of sense of inner worth come between herself and those she walked among, so that there could be the human touching the hunger for which continued in her in spite of everything.

"Which way are you going?"

"It's near the Texaco petrol dump, after the Korle crossing, Doctor."

Normally she would have turned right on leaving the hospital grounds, and less than a mile later the town would have vanished behind her, and all she would have seen would have been the hard dry bush struggling to grow out of the salted-over lagoon earth, an occasional village hidden behind palm branches, and the growing number of new houses with signs outside them saying there was a faith healer living there. But now, when the gleaming infant wing had been left behind, she turned left along the road leading into Accra, a road that used to be wide and free to drive along but had recently been made an awkward trap because someone at the City Council had decided it should be turned into a dual carriageway. All they had done was to run two low cement walls along its length from the hospital entrance to the Korle Lagoon, and the flowers planted between the walls in the first days had very soon become dry brown dust because they were not watered after a while. She would first have to pass through the town she was escaping, and she made up her mind to go along the old shore road leading to the new harbor town at Tema.

Just before they reached the lagoon the air came blowing off it at a tangent and brought sharp whiffs into the car. The nurse giggled in a way that was at once happy and a bit embarrassed, and then she rolled up the window on her side all the way and took special care about locking the little side vent too. Juana looked at her and with some difficulty kept her smile from blowing up into full laughter as she also rolled up her window and closed the side vent.

After the crossing over the Korle Bu Bridge, when she saw the Texaco sign Juana shifted gears and had almost come to a stop when the nurse smiled apologetically and said she had really wanted to get down a little farther on but had found no way of explaining just then. Juana said nothing but drove slowly on until she came to the sign that said NEW TECHNICAL SECONDARY SCHOOL with the building that was to be the school still unfinished though the foundations had already been laid when she first came to this country.

"Here," the nurse said, but Juana had anticipated this suddenness and stopped smoothly, not going too close to the open gutter. The nurse stepped out and said what must have been her long thanks, but the rolled-up glass made it impossible for Juana to hear the words. She just nodded and started the car, reaching out to wave over the top of it.

Juana had come this way for the drive out before, several times, when after long days spent closed in, in the town and the hospital itself, all the boredom and the loneliness and a disgust she could not hold under in spite of all the power of her will, all this created inside her a feeling of attraction, a certain love for being out on the road. Several times, driving along it, letting herself go and pushing the little car to go faster and faster, she could reach back to a feeling that perhaps there would be some meaning waiting for her at the end of a long and aimless drive, that it wasn't true that every important thing that was worthwhile had run slowly out of her life. This need of hers for a periodic escape was in some ways a cure for her own long unease, this leaving Accra to come out for air, with the used portion of the day behind her lined with the wrecked minds it was her job to try and repair, and with the city itself behind her, made as if by some clever mind to produce exactly these wrecks that were her job and such an important, invading part of her own life now. She got angry driving through the town, even with her knowledge of the uselessness of her anger. She got angry whenever she tried to find what use there was in saving people who had found the mess she needed so often to flee from insupportable and had somehow flipped out of it after too much pain too long endured, only to give them the outer toughening they would need so they could be flipped back to get messed up some more in this town that could break any spirit. And then she would catch herself with the knowledge that it was not just the town, that in fact the town was not the worst place. She had been into the countryside and there seen a kind of destruction that made people look to the grinding town as if some salvation could be found there. In the countryside things were worse. So the root of the trouble was deeper.

All the way through James Town, past the prison fort and down the loop past the Post Office, the afternoon traffic had been slow and difficult, and she had not remembered to roll the windows down. It was long after the lagoon had been left behind, after the Post Office where the new Barclay's Bank had gone up on the left opposite the neglected old church just off the shore to the right, and a newer, bigger Standard Bank was rising out in front, that she felt free to roll down both windows all the way. The air that came in was hot and moist with life, and past the silence of Parliament House there was the policeman with his unchanging, incredible happiness and skill directing the traffic just then to a complete stop. The sound of the sea to the right came over with a complete quietness that filled the ear like something made entirely for it, and then in all that heat and wet and peace the happy policeman turned and instead of an arm movement he just winked at her and smiled, and from habit she knew it was his way of telling her her time had come to move. From neutral to first the clutch did not stick at all, amazing thing. The forward move was smooth, and as she touched the rearview mirror, not because it needed adjusting but because she felt the desire to stroke a small itch at the tip of her wedding finger and also to get the sheer feel of the mirror's edge, she could see the policeman telling all those engines with their drivers caught behind them what to do, and she saw that to direct the traffic from behind he seldom needed actually to look behind him, as if he could tell exactly where every vehicle was just from the sounds and the throbbing pulses reaching him there in the center of the road.

Now there was peace in her mind and body and it stayed all along the road past the FREEDOM AND JUSTICE arch monument so that this time she did not think how troubling these words were to a mind that had sought to know what they should mean, how troubling they were in this place. Past the Stadium with the sad and happy football crowds all gone this day, she went left and then dangerously right where the corner was crazy because it had been made that way, and through Christiansborg she slowed down for the many people living there in small spaces and appearing suddenly on the road from behind houses and walls lining it. But she had not intended to stop completely in front of the KALIFONIA MOONBEAM CAFE.

Yet any movement was now impossible. Behind, the line of cars following hers made retreat impossible, and the road forward was at this moment taken. Not by the debris of an accident, not a traffic accident, but by a group of men in government khaki shorts tending with a slow but intense inevitability toward the formation of a circle right there in the road. A few were in singlets but most had bare backs black and glistening with beads of sweat so clear this afternoon they kept the sun's light caught on the men's backs even after they broke and slipped gently down to get absorbed in the lining under government khaki. But the gentleness of the falling of the sweat came out of the harshness of the circle these men were forming, and the concerted strength that filled their beautiful muscles now was born of an immediate and brutal necessity, for Juana saw there, as she looked and followed the line of each man's gaze and the focused tension of the violence no longer hidden in these men's bodies, a shivering dog in the middle of the road. On this hot Atlantic day there was something inside the dog making him so cold he seemed to be searching for the whole feel of the road's warm tar under him, and he was turning round and round in circles trying to reach and touch the tar with every bit of skin he had all in one impossible movement his limbs and bones were not soft enough to give him.

The pain of the dog and all that human tension around him should have made the place loud with noise but there was such a deep quiet even the frightened softness of a small voice begging with a hopeless sound from a child's throat was clearly audible like thin drops falling on hard rock in a desert hot for miles and miles all round. Juana heard the sounds but there was no certainty about their meaning until she asked a woman standing by with her hair not done and her cloth only knotted over her breasts and many signs of hurry in her appearance that said clearly that she had rushed out with sudden speed following the pull of some strange or terrible expectation. The woman spoke a kind of English that was mostly American in sound, and her words were mixed freely with Hausa and Ga and maybe some Fanti words, but the whole stream was clear to Juana in the end, and what she heard was that the child was saying the dog belonged to him and was his best friend in the world, that he had never bitten anyone and was never ever going to bite people and he wasn't a mad dog, only that he was suffering and shivering with coldness because perhaps he had swallowed something bad that he couldn't vomit yet, that he was only a cold dog and would just lie down and soon be warm again if all these strange strong men would leave him alone with his friend.

But apart from the woman with her hair all wild no one else had listened to the meaning of the pleading sounds coming from the child, and the boy, with his mouth pushed awkward in the despair of his fearful begging, suddenly tried to break through the circle of men and reach his dog. The dog was settling for lying on the warm tar with only part of his body, but he was trying to make it his back that touched the warmth and he just couldn't. It seemed he looked in the direction of his friend the boy, but just then he must have seen past something ultimate that burned all hope in him. For one of the men moving in on the dog saw sudden danger in the boy's approach and caught the small frame with all the tension of a grown man's own deep fear and anger, and the child fell from the backward throw with his back scraping the tar at the side of the road where it was covered with browned sand blown off the deep black center tracks by traffic that had gone. The fallen boy made no sound but just lay there. Away from him the circle of men tightened with slow tension around the dog alone. There was no visible hurry on the part of any single man among them to get close to the dog, but the male desire to be the first made all those backs wet with sweat twitch now and then with their own impatient inward heat.

There were . . . how many men? Impossible to tell with any truth, except that they were a lot of men around just one dying dog, and a fear could be seen in them whose strength was strange, seeing that the source of it was such a powerless thing. They had several weapons in their hands, these men. The farthest over was a man with a long head and in his hand he held a cutlass that had in all that sunlight two parts that met along a clear line: the iron back of the weapon was blackened with the safe weathering touch of succeeding rains and drynesses; the twin front end glinted with a beautiful cruel and even delicate steel whiteness as the man swung and shook the whole cutlass, trembling with anticipatory happiness or fear, it was impossible to tell. The next man it seemed had come dreaming straight from some last night's cinema show at the DUNIA or the REGAL or maybe some place far away at the other end of town like the ORBIT. What this dreamer had for a weapon against the suffering dog was a wooden toy molded in the shape of a pistol and painted a luminous color that fascinated the eye in the shining light. And this man too, in his own dreamy state, was in competition with the others to be the first killer of the dog. He had long hairy legs and even when he tried to frown most fiercely at the shivering dog his mouth betrayed him with something close to sympathy perhaps: a look that was funny and sly and still remained as serious as the muteness on the mouth of the dog himself.

Then there was a man with a torn singlet that had grown brown and through which his belly pushed into the open world, and it was not a small belly. He had a pitchfork held in both hands one middle tooth of which was broken where it should have started, and the black and the white of his eyes shone intensely with a devouring desire to fix the dog lying there. There were others, but they stood out from the human rest neither in any great personal peculiarity nor in any markedly higher boldness in the way in which they intended to murder their victim dog.

Except one. He was a short man, with something swollen and out of shape about his shortness, so that the eye on first seeing him searched unordered for some twisting cause, for something perhaps like a hump upon his back. But there was nothing there to explain the twistedness, until the baffled eye descended and was struck in the region of the sweating man's loins with the sight of a scrotal sac so swollen that within the tattered pants containing it it had the look of a third and larger buttock winning a ruthless struggle to push the original two out of the way.

Now as the powerful human group not only tightened around the dying dog but also shifted in an unconscious circle, this last man also moved inward and around till he too in his turn was opposite, and Juana saw in his eyes a manic shine with far more burn in it than that possessing any of the others, and she knew at once that this was a man who needed something like the first killing of the dog for reasons that lay within and were far more powerful than the mere outside glory open to the hunter with his kill.

There was not much distance left between the hunters and their prey. It seemed only fear kept any man within the circle from the striking of a precipitate, uncertain blow. But the man with the swollen scrotum had by now maneuvered himself into a position just behind the dog's head. A long shout from the man with the broken pitchfork told the rest in pidgin to be careful: a bite from a mad dog about to die would surely send the bitten man to death after many kinds of suffering of which it would be better not to speak. As this shout rose and died the man with the swollen scrotum raised his weapon high toward the sun: it was a pickax with a handle made lean in the middle but thickening toward the ends to fit the hole in the metal head and the opening made by grasping human hands.

The way in which the eager, fearful carefulness of the whole circle was broken by the descent of the last man's pickax was so swift and so sudden that even though the blow had been expected, it still surprised the watching eye, and the trueness of its aim was uncanny. For the point of the implement went in not far from the exact middle of the dog's head. In the first few moments nothing happened save for a twitching movement – it could have been of joy or of fear – that ran down the tight body of the man who had shattered the dog's life. That, and a whimper barely audible, a sound expressing not surpassed sadness but a final acceptance, and it came from the boy who had tried so impotently to save his friend.

Then around the buried point of the weapon the dog's life began its final coming. It was white at first, the matter of the animal's brains, then blood mixed it with a tentative light brown that deepened into red with a stronger flow. In the middle of the road the white ooze reached the black tar before the red blood, now that it had begun to spurt, first joined and then covered everything around the pierced head.

The last man with the swollen sac was twitching no longer.

Instead, with a shout that was abrupt and high he twisted his pickax cleverly so that the dog's head did not slip from it, and then he raised the whole high up in victory. The other men parted, each drawing back to make way for him. All watched him with the tension now gone low in their bodies and the sweat now beginning to dry and to leave faint salt streaks on them. The circle broke in silence, and the men who had formed it strained almost involuntarily, following the last man who had become the first to kill the dog, first with their eyes, and then bodily walking after him.

The triumphant killer walked off with his prize in a strange way, as if it were his intention to go through all the motions of a runner while keeping a walker's speed. The drip of life came down from the upturned end of the pickax. But from the man himself something else had commenced to drip: down along his right leg flowed a stream of something yellow like long-thickened urine mixed with streaks of clotted blood. A look of terror stopped the man's triumph as first he felt the drip and then looked down to see what it could be. The fallen child had risen. Seeing the humiliation of the killer of his dog, he was now shouting, laughing through his tears,

"Fat balls, hei!"

The boy was still weeping, and the shout had turned his silent grief into a hysterical mixture of suffering for his lost dog and mockery of the killer. But for the killer himself, a wild feeling of relief seemed to have come in place of the first, short fear. Something that had stayed locked up and poisoned the masculinity of his days was now coming down, and in spite of all his shame he seemed seized by an uncontrollable happiness that made him walk with the high, proud, exaggerated steps of a puppet.

"Hei, *tilati*, hei, hei!" the boy shouted again.

The woman from the KALIFONIA MOONBEAM CAFE looked contemptuously at the dripping man and at the other members of his now broken circle moving away, and she spat a long stream of spittle after them.

"Killers," she said, making no attempt to shout. "Killers, and all they wanted was a meal."

A new access of sobbing took hold of the boy and he began again his long weeping explanation to which none of the men had listened. There was no hysteria now, neither weeping nor laughter.

Now that the road was clear an impatient honk came from

somewhere behind, and several other cars took up the sound and filled the air with it. A Shell tanker had stopped with all its length and huge bulk in the dead middle of the road. Passing it was impossible, except for one man on a Honda who threaded his way past all the drivers trapped in the cars behind the tanker, smiling wickedly and waving at them all. When he passed by Juana he turned to take a second closer look. She waved back, and with a very satisfied grin he rode off. Then the tanker moved at last, the cars behind it started, and Juana took her place in the line of traffic going out of the city. Drivers in a hurry, driving mostly new white Mercedes or light gray Peugeot cars, sped angrily by trying to get past the long Shell tanker in front. Juana let them pass, going slowly, looking at the life that lined the roadside. Where the road began opening out, half a mile past the last of the petrol stations, was a shut-down distillery – the end of someone's dream.

A man drove by with a speed whose sureness indicated a complete trust in the machine under his control. His car swung out past two cars, hesitated a moment behind the Shell tanker before squeezing past it calculated seconds before a green Mercedes bus came the opposite way. The two cars ahead also moved out past the tanker, leaving Juana directly behind it. Through Teshie, past the Military Range with its distant numbered practice targets and the sea beyond it still blue and beautiful, the road remained wide and the traffic was fast, but still people crossed, and once a pair of young eyes stared hard through her advancing windscreen at Juana, and the eyes had in them both a simple defiance and also something close to a precocious knowledge that a sudden violent death would not be such a bad thing after all.

Around a corner out front Juana just had the time to see a small india-rubber ball bounce swiftly across the road in front of the Shell tanker and then in a reflex reaction she pressed hard on her brake as a child ran after the ball, knowing nothing of the huge vehicle's advance. Juana only heard the noise as the tanker shuddered with a brutal suddenness to a stop. When she was able to open her eyes again she saw the child still running, but with a terrified slowness now, and when he tried to leap over the open drain at the side of the road he missed the other lip and fell hard against the mossy side. From the tanker the angry driver had descended and was advancing toward the child, and not with love. But before the driver could get to him the child had scrambled over the gutter's edge. From the nearest house a woman emerged, her hands dripping red with the palm oil of her cooking. The child leaped at her whimpering and burying his face in the cloth over her belly, and she held him hard against herself, the veins on her hands and neck standing out with the palpitation of her fear. The driver advanced relentlessly, his anger plain on his face, till the mother saw him and began to beg.

"*Owura* driver," she said in Akan, and Juana strained to understand, "forgive him. He's a child. Perhaps you have one like him. *Owura*, forgive him, he doesn't know."

The mother's face was twisted with her anxiety, but through it she managed to force a smile to sweeten the temper of the angry man. But suddenly the driver seemed to have forgotten about the child, and his anger brought on a scowl of contempt.

"And you," he said with a slowness intended to wound, "are you a woman and a mother? What kind of mother, that you leave your own child out, to play with death? What kind of woman are you?"

The difficult smile did not go from the woman's face. "Yes I beg your forgiveness for myself also, but spare him. He is only a child."

"And you are a foolish woman!" the driver shouted.

"Yes, *Owura* driver," the woman said. "Insult me. I will accept your abuse for the gift of his life." The smile had gone now, but in its place there was no answering anger, only a sober, accepting look. "His father works. In Tema. He comes late, and he must eat. I must cook. I must wash. And the child. What can I say to him when he wants to play?"

"You should have thought of that before you spread your thighs apart." The driver turned, walked with a tense calmness across the road, and climbed up into his high seat.

"Insult me, *Owura*," the woman continued saying. "So long as I have his little life, insult me. There is hope."

The driver started his engine and the tanker roared off. Then the woman's face hardened as she looked down at her child and she began asking angry scolding questions, but midstream her harshness broke and turned instead into an inquiry that sounded long and very loving and was filled with a palpable wonder. She seemed flooded with something coming from inside herself, and she shook with the emotion of her own silent crying, tears dropping freely and slipping down the black arms of the child.

When Juana started again, her thoughts were of salvation. A

mood, perhaps, brought on by the near-accident. She had seen the mother's fear of something so nearly final, and in herself she had felt something of the tremendous luck of the moment, when the mother had trembled with all that sorrow for what could have happened and with gratitude that it had not. And then the resolve to take care from the lucky moment of salvation onward, but the last thing she said had brought out her knowing fear of the immensity of the long hazard ahead.

"This life," she had said, looking down from the sky at her child with the tears falling more slowly, shaking her head. This life. All the woman knew. A long stretch of danger with both ends unknown, the only certain things being the constant threat and the presence of loss on a way lined with infrequent, brief, unlikely hopes and once in a long while such unexpected miracle escapes from the edge of the unknown.

Again, the question rose to force the direction of her thoughts: whether all this was worth anything. What meaning could hope have in an environment so completely seized with danger and so many different kinds of loss? It was too widely spread, the damage. Even of physical destruction, of broken bodies, the town was a prolific creator. The thing that made such small saving attempts as she was capable of unreal was the magnitude of the need, and the far greater magnitude of other, more immediate needs. But then such thoughts had no rest in them. It takes a huge amount of energy to drive a human mind against points hard enough to fracture it. More to solder it. Where then was the justification for the long effort to push back into this life those who had found it harder than the woman and had fallen down into things set deeper within themselves? What justification for sending the once destroyed back to knock again against the very things that had destroyed their peace? It had been possible to think of abstract things, of comparisons, of environments and types of adaptation. Until coming out from behind the mosquito screens of government bungalows one actually went into the environment and saw life lived not with it but of necessity *against* it. Until such knowledge the life here, the thick suffocating rumors that filled long lines of weeks, the news itself that appeared in the government papers, all this was too strange, too hopelessly bizarre, for comprehension. Once a small item in the *National Times* had mentioned the arrest of two men for wearing T-shirts with cartoons of sweating wrestlers on them under the printed caption

STRUGGLERS!

Too bold, an editorial the following day had called the T-shirts and the words on them. What purpose, demanded the editor, could such images and words have, save to trouble the peaceful minds of hardworking citizens with a view to subverting the nation as a whole?

On every journey Juana had passed and been passed by many lorries and little Mercedes buses bearing the sign

OBRA YE KO.

One of the first things she had done, on beginning to learn Akan, was to ask what the signs meant. Oh, nothing, just life is war, she was told. There were other signs, cryptic to her until with time she asked and reached the realization that these were signs and words that had grown all too naturally from the place itself and the people here.

She had learned the meaning of another sign when, sick of the quickly worn circuit to which the expatriate crowd kept, from bungalow to work to ingrown parties to nights at the Star after evenings spent chatting with visitors in embassies or at the Ambassador Hotel, to weekends on beaches or in the sun beside the new pool at Akosombo, she had stopped listening to what strangers said about the place and the people and started looking and asking herself. SMOG. Save Me Oh God. The explainer had laughed that time too, long enough to make her ask why.

"Is funny, no?" The explainer was the driver of one such bus bearing the sign. "Poor man never get bank account. But he look far in de sky and he tink in him he get some last chance. In heaven."

The cryptic signs now made too much sense, and the strangeness of the place all vanished. This was life. But there were always newcomers passing through, who looked at everything and said how picturesque and beautiful it was. They were right. Only the surface was visible to them, and the sun here could make anything shine. But then at first, with the opening out of her own mind to accept the place she had come to, Juana had found it difficult to understand the willingness with which the expatriates kept themselves imprisoned in their little blind incestuous groups. With more looking and understanding she saw it was not really blindness, but a decision quite consciously made not to see, or to see but never to let any real understanding intrude. The expatriates could see the damnation of the ones outside their bored circles. They could talk about it to spice dull dinners, turning the absurdity of the life that had trapped their hosts into laughing matter. And the one or two who somehow found their way to the meaning and the suffering found their food turning bitter in their mouths, retreated into silence and left the place as soon as possible. For what other apparent sanctuaries from life?

As for the people here themselves, they knew. Once during a break Juana had come out to find the nurse Patience arguing with an Assistant from the new Psychiatric Laboratory. His name was Bukari, and it seemed he had said something about the patients being like fish out of water.

"It's their own fault," Patience was saying. "The things they do. They're too adventurous." The word was surprising.

"How, adventurous?"

"You have seen them. Drinkers, wee smokers, occultists, all the strange things they do."

"They first try to find a way out themselves, out of a bad life," Bukari said.

"Well," said Patience, "they succeed in falling out. You are right, then. They're fish out of water."

"Yes. Fish out of water, all these cases. Fish out of water." Bukari was nodding quietly, as if this truth had completely defeated him. Juana was getting back into the consultation room, about to close the door behind her when she heard the last faint words on which Bukari ended his head-shaking acceptance: ". . . out of water, yes. Boiling water."

The road was completely open. Juana drove past the last of the military warning notices, through a gap cut in the low hill, followed the road right almost to the beach itself, then left again and straight east toward Tema. The road lay so close to the sea that in places past rains had eaten deep gullies in the earth, turning it to sand. The breezes had left sand blowing in swirling cresent patterns all the way along the right side of the road. Coconut trees lined the half-firm land between the road and the shore, their leaves gently wind-blown with every swell in the breeze. A dead branch hung with its long leaves brown and stiff with dryness, the trees themselves casting shadows slanted toward the sea, falling across the sand in dark long parallel lines that sometimes merged by accident with other coconut trees.

The road turned up left again, going over an iron bridge rusty with wet salt, with the old Tema construction sidetrack passing underneath in a straight double line. The black tar swung more sharply left to avoid the small lagoon on the right with the rail line riding between it and the sea on a raised causeway. The lines looked brown with rust and completely deserted now that Tema was a finished thing and no trains passed this way anymore.

After the lagoon the road dipped back toward the sea, then stayed on a straight course. The car swayed slightly left with the sudden strengthening of the breeze from the sea. Juana was now close to the Shell tanker, and it was moving with an increasingly irritating slowness. She honked and got ready to drive past. She could see no sign from the cab of the tanker. When she was half way past its long length, the driver swerved suddenly right into the center of the road. Simultaneously he began to accelerate. From the distance ahead a light brown lorry appeared, coming on fast. By now she had drawn level with the Shell driver, but the man was accelerating steadily, looking sullenly ahead. She decelerated sharply. She waited for the length of the tanker to pass her by on the left, and moved over to the left side of the road just in time to avoid the hurtling lorry.

The suddenness with which slowness had been forced on her turned her mind to asking why she had found her speed so necessary and so enjoyable. She thought the answer would have something to do with the fact of thinking less and seeing less while driving slowly, but there was no time now to follow these thoughts.

Up ahead, she saw a dirt track turn left off the main road. By the time she reached it she had made up her mind to go up it. At first the track bed was of smooth red laterite, recently pressed down. But abruptly it degenerated into a stretch of sharp pebbles that flew apart with the car's advance, and even this was replaced by long gullies and large dangerous stones, plus here and there the still visible marks of heavy trucks and caterpillars. After a sharp climb she stopped the car in a small clearing. The road seemed to have stopped nowhere, but when she looked round she saw the dug-out remains of an old stone quarry.

Around her the vegetation was not forest, but it was high enough to block her view. It was mostly planted crops, crawling ground-nuts, cassava now grown high, and here and there the huge wild leaves of a cocoyam plant. She moved along a path crossing the groundnuts. When she came to the end of it she walked along the edge of the cassava stands till she came to another path leading down from the hill. In a while the sea was visible again. Not the shore and the surf, which at that distance were still hidden by the coconuts and the vegetation close by. But against a clear horizon the whole expanse of the sea was visible, and from the hill it seemed so immediately close that for a moment Juana felt she could take one vertical step and fall straight down into it. From time to time the planted vegetation and the tall reeds parted and revealed not only the sea but a ship on it, white and solitary but looking very close. An infantile illusion, this closeness, Juana knew, thinking of forgotten days back home when she had run from her mother's restraining hold thinking she was going down to find this time a ship really touchable on the shore. Even now the urge was not entirely dead, in spite of knowledge and the passage of years.

The undergrowth was thick, and was often hidden to her beneath grass and creepers and fungoid growths taking over once again their earth. Juana lost the path, found it several times again in its continuation farther on, then lost it again when she came to the clearing that was a second farm. It had low cassava stems stuck slanting into the flat earth and mounds of earth serving as beds for heads of yams with hopeful poles stuck in for climbers yet to appear from the red-brown laterite heaps packed with light pebbles and broken lumps of sandstone. Across the clearing Juana had to walk sideways against the steepness of the slope. Sand got into her sandals, and once a sharp lump forced her to stop. When she took it out she saw it was a broken-off piece of a pebble with a spot of her blood on it.

She threw the stone away and, straightening up, saw just along the path a single flower on a stalk that stood up slender almost like a vine. It was yellow. In all the green around and among all the tall reeds, there was nothing else like that flower. Coming across the line of her vision, a bird whose color was a smooth black shading with no visible lines of transition into red, flew noiselessly and came to rest on the flower. She thought the stalk would break or at least bend a long way down, it looked so fragile; but incredibly, it bent only slightly. The impulse to touch that smooth beauty grew strong in her, and she approached the flower quietly, hoping to draw near without frightening the bird. But before she could take more than a few steps the bird flew upward, hovered almost without any motion just above the greenness, then darted swiftly sideways to settle on a reed more safely out of reach.

The descent was faster now, and easier. The soil was sandier, and only a few cassava stems stuck out of it at intervals that increased until, getting to the side of the road, there was nothing but sandy soil and stones. Juana took her time, waiting for a long gap in the traffic. After the vehicles had passed, while she was crossing the road, she looked down and saw traces of new sand where it had just been pressed into the tar, and she kept looking back at the road even when she had crossed it and was making for the beach. The breeze gained a sudden brief strength and turned into wind that whistled through the coconut leaves and swept fresh sand toward the shiny black middle of the road in curling ears, the farthest sweeps thinning till the last grains, isolated and almost without weight, rose with the small dying swells of the wind and fell again farther along the road, bouncing and then coming to rest, single grains parted from other sand. A truck passed on its way to Tema, and it scattered some of the new grains again and pressed those directly in its path into the tar. The coconut leaves brushed against each other and their parent trunks with an unhurried rhythm, and in the lull Juana caught the far-off sounds of a unison chant that was hot and religious, and two brief jangles of a joyful tambourine.

Now that she was on the beach itself, she looked out over the expanse of the sea. There was a ship, but it was far away, and every moment made it inexorably smaller and added distance. The illusion and its dissipation were not new to Juana. They were only new reminders of old childish disappointments, coming to her like so many other things here that could very easily be copies or originals of sights she had left behind. With these reminders everywhere there was little hope of any peace to be found in constant movement. There would only be a restlessness whose pain never ended but got dissolved in the knowledge that the fugitive could never leave the causes of her pain behind. The causes would burrow inward, travel along everywhere with the carrying mind, and mix their old traces with the sights and sounds of every new place the traveler came to.

Juana kept her sandals on till she came to the waterline where the sand was not so hot because the surf washed up all the way and gave it a cool firmness. The music of voices and tambourines was no longer intermittent. It came in waves that grew stonger as she walked along the edge of the surf, keeping just out of reach of the farthest fingers of every fresh wave. A few yards upward to her right the sand was thoroughly disturbed where dozens of feet had trampled it, going up a rise just ahead of her. When she herself came to the rise she saw the makers of the footprints and the sounds.

They were about a quarter of a mile away, a group numbering easily over a hundred. They were singing, and all swaying in time with their music except that now and then an arm shot out above all those heads and shook a shiny tambourine. The group stood packed together away from the sea, but they seemed completely unmindful of the heat of the sand underfoot. Seaward from them, standing where the sand was cool and the waves still gently frothy around his feet, a man with a thick beard and a long white robe gesticulated, danced and swayed with the music, and kept it going till he himself seemed exhausted. Then he raised his hand and brought it suddenly down, and with a swift obedience the singing and the tinkling of tambourine bells all stopped, and only the breeze from the sea was to be heard. The bearded man beckoned in a movement that was filled with his sureness of his own authority. A woman detached herself and drew near him. He stopped her at the point where the hot sand met the wet, and began to speak to his followers. The woman in the middle translated the words, for the preacher's message was in English. Juana was close enough to hear the English words, and it pleased her also to know how much of the Akan was readily comprehensible to her now. The bearded man in his white robe spoke mainly of fire. Different kinds of fire, fire from the Old Testament Bible, the fire of God's anger and his glory, matched with the burning unending fire of the devil in his hell, and as the message got to them his hearers groaned in their despair and sweated where they stood out there with the hot sand underfoot. Then the message turned sweet with the promise of rest and the cool peace of heaven waiting for the good, and now cries of "Jesus! Oh JESUS!" broke from suffering throats. Two women screamed deliriously and in a frenzy tore their own clothes to bits, then lay down in the burning sand and began rolling naked to the sea. A man moved to stop them, but the bearded man in his long white robe raised a commanding hand and at the same time shouted loud enough so that even above the general noise his words were clearly heard.

"Come to me!" he said. "Let them come to me!" The man who had moved regained the group. "Come to me, all of you! Come to me in the nakedness of your first days!"

The shout was followed immediately by a long wail filled with suffering and desire, rising as if by prior agreement from almost all those throats, tearing the air. At the same time more women dropped their clothes, and the group that had stood and chanted became a mass of human flesh and limbs rolling in the sand and sending cries up toward the sky. The bearded man, with the help of two men, waited for the rolling women to reach him, then with each incoming wave from the sea he held each roller's head beneath the water a number of seconds, then left the body in his helpers' hands while he seized another naked woman for the holy rite.

Juana put her sandals back on and skirted the group, then walked on west. From time to time she looked back over her shoulder and saw the worshipers, now exhausted, successively rolling to a rest in the dry sand.

Over in the far distance, she could see the white form, very small at this distance, of the old slave castle which had now become the proud seat of the new rulers, the blind children of slavery themselves. She knew it was no use asking anyone any questions about that. No one seemed to need forgiveness, and it was no use feeling sorry for oneself, for crimes borne by people with whom one identified. The real crime now was the ignorance of past crime, and that, it seemed, would be a permanent sort of ignorance in places like this and places like home. How lean things were around her: the tall lean coconut trees with their shadows elongated by the sun, crabs with long, lean legs disappearing down small holes at her approach.

What a curse it was to have the constant remembrance of a time when youth was not something one had lived through, not just a defeated thought, but the hope of consant regeneration, the daring to reach out toward a new world. Life then had taken its color from the brilliance of an always imminent apocalypse, and if the beautiful colors were mixed with the red of blood and the sulfurous yellow flames, that was in no way a reason to run from the dream. The burning of old frames and the shedding of cruel blood would not be against the making of another world. Life had a charge, and every day's efforts had at their end the hope that things dreamed of had been brought closer. Now she was getting used to continuing without the steam and the charge. It should have been easy to cut disturbing dreams down to the size of the self alone, to walk in peace here when despair threatened, in the sun and shadows beneath the coconut trees, and to look at the light shaken by the movement of the sea. There were things here that could also suggest the message of peace, if only the inner turbulence would find a way to die.

The first months here had been terrible for a mind that had come prepared to find its own part in a struggle assumed to be going on. But watching and listening, moving and learning what life was about in this place, she had understood that what she had thought she would find was not here at all. None of the struggle, none of the fire of defiance; just the living defeat of whole peoples – the familiar fabric of her life. After such an understanding, peace should perhaps have come, but that was also impossible, with so many reminders around of the impotence of victims and of the blindness of those who had risen to guide them. She had learned ways of making the necessary peace for herself. Adjustment. Something necessary and true, though she had gotten into the habit of laughing at the bald word itself. A matter of knowing what visions people lead their lives by, or by what visions life leads them. And survival. A matter of adopting a narrower vision every time the full vision threatens danger to the visionary self.

The small form of the distant castle brought memories, and again her doubts returned: why had she really come here? When would she make the decision about leaving or staying? What sense would there be in a final decision to stay now that she knew there were people here who knew of the awfulness of the life around them, who had the power given them to do something to change all this, but who were, like people she had known at home and in all her travels, only concerned with digging themselves a comfortable resting place within a bad system? People with their eyes deliberately closed against the knowledge that their own useless lives were part of the slow dissolution of their peoples, doomed to an extinction started long ago. It had been so strange, sitting after midnight one nearly forgotten day when the newness was still there, watching the dreamy dancers flow like bound people round the circle of the dance floor at the Star; with the desire to find sleep far from her mind, it had been strange to ask for the meaning of the new Ramblers' song, and to have the smiling young Ghanaian doctor who was her partner say calmly to her,

> Happy are those whose life is today
> and only today.
> Sad are the prophets
> and those others whose eyes are open to the past.
> Blessed are they who neither see their painful yesterdays
> nor their tomorrows filled with despair:
> They shall rest in peace.

It hadn't been so long ago, but many events had happened, and things had risen to the surface in her own mind and around her which tended always toward the disturbing sensation that even the small areas of personal peace would not last long.

In the distance, moving toward her, she saw a group of young men, five or six. It would be good to walk without fear among a people she had wished to live with as her own, but these days were full of so much violence used in the hope of stealing so little, that she too had come to accept as permanent a violence directed only against the weak, and to seek refuge in distrust and flight. She turned back. The group seemed to be gaining on her, till she began running toward the prophet and his followers, and then the young men stopped and lay down upon the sand.

Before Juana came to the worshipers the prophet had finished a last speech and the gathering had started breaking up. In little bands they climbed up the sand to wait by the roadside to get on small buses returning from Tema to Accra. After the third bus the prophet said farewell to those remaining and moved with the two men who had helped him at the water's edge, the woman who had translated his words into Akan, and two other women, toward a light blue Mercedes parked among the coconut trees farther down. Juana had not noticed the car. When it took off she noticed the prophet was not driving it. One of his helpers was acting as the chauffeur.

The waiting worshipers thinned out as more buses came and went. Juana was thinking of going back herself when she noticed one of the prophet's followers. She was not waiting with the others by the road, but sitting on the beach with her back curved against the convex side of a big timber log stranded out of the water's reach. She had her legs spread out in front of her, and as Juana approached her she thought her eyes were closed against the sun. Her clothes showed no signs of having been taken off on the beach and put back on, and her eyes must have been only half shut, because it was she who greeted Juana, in English. The woman looked not yet fifty but long past forty and still beautiful with teeth that shone white when she spoke or smiled. When Juana answered her greeting she began a conversation with an eagerness that had at the same time something girlish and something very coquettish in it.

"You are an Afro-American," the woman said.

"Puerto Rican," Juana answered.

"What does that mean?"

"Something like the same thing, really. I have spent most of my life in America, and some of my people also came from here. And you?"

"I have never traveled anywhere," the woman said. She drew her shawl, made of the same green fabric as her cloth and blouse, closer around her shoulders, but the wind lifted it again and made it hang with a look of pretty negligence from one shoulder only. "Oh, I have made small journeys, but always here in this country. I was born here and have never been anywhere. Except twice to Togo."

"Do you come here often?"

"You mean with the prophet? This is my first time."

"Will you continue?"

"Come and sit down," the woman said, smoothing out the sand beside her. Juana sat. "Yes, I will continue following him, if it is true . . ."

"If what it true?"

"If I get what I want. The prophet has promised me something, if only I have faith and follow him."

"Is it a secret, the thing he has promised you?"

The woman smiled, very coyly. "Perhaps you know," she said.

"Money?" Juana guessed.

"Ah, everybody wants money. But that is not why I came to the prophet. Not yet, anyway."

"A husband?"

"Ei! You know many of the reasons why people come to the

prophet." The smile was even coyer now. "But I am not a young girl anymore, though I can tell you that some men . . ." She winked at Juana.

"A child?" Juana asked, winking back. The woman's answer surprised her.

"Something like that." She did not seem about to continue, but Juana could not prevent her from seeing her puzzled look, and in a while she added, "I know what you are thinking. I think you are thinking I'm a strange woman because I want a child."

"Well —" Juana could not find the evasive words she sought — "at home too, where I come from, our people will do anything to get a child."

"Children are the most important things in this life," the woman answered, giving the statement the quiet finality of truths held to be self-evident.

"And you don't have any?" Juana asked.

The woman again caught her wind-blown shawl, rearranged it over her shoulders, and then held up three fingers of her right hand for Juana to see. "You don't understand," she said. "I have had three children. One died young. The child I am waiting for is not new. He is — let me see — now twenty-five. No, that's his school age. Twenty-six, really."

"He's left?"

"Oh —" the woman touched her belly gently — "he went away to study. He will come back a man. A big man." She turned round and looked over the timber log, out at the sea. Pointing, she said, "He will be coming from over there, or out of the sky, in a plane." She paused; then, as if this was something that needed to come out, like breath, she added, "Five years. It's five years since he went away, and I have been fearing he was totally lost."

Juana smiled and said, "A mother's fears —" She was cut short.

"No. He did not want to come back."

"Why not?"

"I do not understand," the woman said, and her eyes had begun to fill with tears. "I cannot understand. All my hopes went with him, and he was going to leave me here, like an old woman on the shore, struggling to take my snuff in a hurricane." Her tears stayed unshed, and she smiled. "Because of him I have come to the prophet. I have prayed harder than any woman who has lost her most precious trinkets, and I do not want to tempt God, but I think my prayers are soon to be answered."

"You have had good news?"

"He has written, and he is coming. I don't know when. He didn't say. He would be here by now, but he fell very ill."

"What's his name?"

"Baako."

"You know nothing of his illness?"

"Nothing," said the woman, shaking her head. "Nothing. It has been confusing. They say there was nothing wrong with his body. The prophet says it was a sickness of the soul, sent by God to bring my lost one back to me."

"You believe the prophet."

"Not everything he says. But about my son, I must believe him."

"Where did he go?"

"America."

"I see." Juana looked up, and found herself having to squint against the descending sun.

"Tell me," the woman said, "what is there that so many of our young people go there and do not want to return? I am not the only one."

"I don't know," Juana answered. "You think it is something there holding him?"

"What else could it be?"

"Things here he is afraid to come back to?"

The woman ignored the query completely, filling the silence after it with a long sigh. Then, as if it was something new that had struck her, she said, "I hope he comes, that's all. Soon." She got up and nodded in the direction of the road, then began walking away.

"You must love your son very much," Juana said after her, but she had not shouted the words, and the wind carried them away. The woman had not heard, but suddenly Juana saw her stop. She was saying something, but against the wind the sound of her words was inaudible. Juana strained to hear her, then gave up and moved toward the woman where she had stopped.

"I could not hear you," Juana said.

"I was asking where you worked. Perhaps I will come and see you one day."

"Korle Bu Hospital. The new wing."

"It's so beautiful," the woman said. Juana smiled. "You are a doctor?"

"A psychiatrist, yes."

When the two came to the first row of coconut trees the woman stopped to pick up a yellowish leaf, freshly fallen. She separated the long, hard spine, broke it near its base and put the smaller piece in between her teeth. At the roadside the last of the remaining worshipers were climbing into a small Datsun bus that had just stopped. The woman looked uncertainly after them.

"I'll drive you into town," Juana said. Her companion smiled and thanked her. "I left my car up on that hill. I'm going up to get it. You can wait here for me."

"I can climb up with you."

"It's a steep climb," Juana said.

The woman laughed. "I should be saying that to you."

But by the time they got to the car, Juana was the less winded of the two, and the woman, when she opened the door for her, sat down and sighed gratefully, breathing heavily while Juana turned the car round.

"Where do you live?" she asked.

"Kaneshie," the other said. "But you can drop me anywhere in town, and I'll wait for a bus."

"The buses are slow here."

"I know. Some never come."

"I'll take you home. It's only two miles from Kaneshie to Korle Bu," Juana said.

There was not much traffic on the way back. Even the Circle looked a bit deserted, and along the cemetery road into Kaneshie not a single car passed. Juana drove slowly, prompting the woman for further instructions at every turning. Each time, she saw her retreat into a sort of absentminded dream immediately after telling her where next to turn.

"There!" the woman said finally, pointing to a low house with a red roof and a white wall surrounding it.

"It's a pretty house," Juana said, stopping at the gate.

"Do you think so?" the woman asked eagerly. "Do you really think it will be good enough for a been-to?"

Juana did not know what to say. She smiled self-consciously and said again, "I hope your son returns soon."

"Oh, I hope so too, with all my soul." She closed the door, too softly, so that Juana had to reach over and shut it more firmly. As the woman walked to her gate she looked back and thanked Juana again.

"You told me your son's name," Juana half shouted after her, "but I still don't know yours."

"Efua," the woman said, coming closer. "And you, Doctor?"

"Juana."

"Doctor Juana."

"No. Just Juana. Doctor isn't my name. It's just my job."

The woman's smile turned into open laughter, and she waved to Juana all the way till she turned the Link Road corner and made for the West Ring Road intersection. She did not feel tired, or sad. The safe confusing numbness had returned, and she drove at an even speed along the familiar way back to the hospital.

3 : Akwaaba

WHEN THE AIRPORT BUS came to a stop, slanted into a slot beside four others, Baako avoided the initial stampede of passengers in a hurry. When the press had eased he rose and picked up his luggage — suitcase, portable typewriter and guitar — and went down the bus steps, turning slightly sideways to get through the door. The hazed green glass windows of the bus had given the light outside a certain dark softness. Abruptly this quality had changed to a klieg intensity that gave the atmosphere around something of a bleached, ashen quality and made even the warmth of the afternoon feel deceptively cool. Ahead, a woman with her hair gone completely white emerged pushing a trolley with two blade-blue suitcases on it onto the sidewalk and right toward a short line of taxis. When she had gone Baako put his luggage on the empty trolley and pushed it to the next door marked ENTRÉE — IN. The wheels of the trolley touched the black rubber apron in front of the entrance, the glass doors swung in away from him and he walked into the long building.

Inside, the light coming through the long glass walls did not seem to have lost any of its high intensity. If anything, the parallel lines of fluorescent tubes running overhead increased it, filling the air with a surfeit of whiteness.

Baako scanned the airway counters along the wall on the right and pushed his trolley over to one over which the illuminated sign said

AIR AFRIQUE.

Behind it sat two girls in blue-gray uniform. One of them was black and wore a wig that had a single bleached strand leading its general dark brown mass. The other was a lean blonde who sat there staring absently ahead with her lower lip caught firmly between her teeth.

When Baako drew opposite the blonde he checked the trolley's slide and asked her, "Do you speak English?" The girl indicated the black one did, and Baako moved over.

"I have a ticket that I got changed at the Invalides." He held out the ticket, and the black girl took it and studied it.

"New York, Paris," she said softly. "Ah, Paris, Accra. Yes, there is a flight at sixteen hours forty-five minutes. Passengers will be called at sixteen hours fifteen minutes."

"Where do I go?"

"Straight down here," she pointed down the length of the building. "When you come to the clock, follow the arrow. After the point of rendezvous, there, you will find the entrance to the Customs upstairs. You can check your baggage here."

Baako took his suitcase out of the trolley and placed it on the low scale beside the counter.

"And the instrument?" the girl asked, looking at the pointer on the scale. "Your bag is not very heavy."

"I know," Baako said, "but I think I'd better keep my guitar with me."

"You are afraid it will be broken?" The girl shook her head and smiled. "It will be safe."

"O.K." Baako placed the guitar beside his suitcase. The girl tilted her head to look at the pointer.

"Perfect," she smiled.

Baako smiled back, thanked her, and pushed the trolley left toward a row of several more like it near one of the doors. When he was almost at the door he took out the typewriter and pushed the trolley carefully. It rolled forward and got telescoped into the last. He walked to the luminous dial and followed its arrow right. Some ten yards to the left another line of counters began, stretching away into the interior distance. In the space between the two sets of counters a polished aluminum globe revolved slowly, suspended in the center. A white equatorial band circled it, showing the blue lettering on it that said alternately,

POINT DE RENCONTRE   RENDEZVOUS POINT.

Long red benches formed a low square behind the globe. Baako found an empty place facing the globe with the outside light behind it and sat looking at the thin rods descending from the globe, with small, discreetly polished and slightly curved panels, also of aluminum, wrapped at staggered intervals around them.

Watching the turning globe and listening to the occasional glad exclamations that broke the soft, indeterminate talk around him, he felt the vague nausea threatening to return, weaker this time but still unsettling, starting with a tightening sensation somewhere near the top and back of his skull. He closed his eyes, but that only made the feeling worse. Opening them, he rose and took a few steps past the globe, looking for the dial. The clock said 3:52. He walked back to his seat, picked up the typewriter and went to the check point at the bottom of the escalators. The guard looked at his ticket, asked to see his passport, gave both back after a cursory examination, and let him through.

Past shiny invitations to a row of elevators and a bar, Baako took a second escalator. A panel at the bottom had promised an art gallery here, but there was only a small maze of bright, empty display boards under the acoustic-tiled ceiling. Beyond the escalators another sign advertised a restaurant open on the floor above:

LES TROIS SOLEILS.

The brilliance of the letters was reflected in the polished floor. Walking round the display boards, Baako found himself listening to the soft sound of falling water, then looking at an indoor waterfall with the water at the bottom illuminated from below. Big hunks of dead wood had been arranged in the water to create an illusion of tropicality. Where the wood stood out of the water it had gone a dry, powdery white; but the immersed portions made brown and yellow patterns with the mixture of light and water that made the illusion begin to look alive. Baako placed his typewriter near the pool's edge and bent to touch the water. It was cold, but just behind the biggest log two live ducks were slowly, almost imperceptibly, moving in it as if the cold light from below gave them heat enough. One of them climbed onto the side of the pool, leaving the other alone, and the momentary violence of its motion fractured the shimmering light over the stones at the bottom of the water. Sitting on the containing ledge, Baako watched the two ducks and the logs with the water shaking and falling around and behind them, looking at the ceiling reflected beneath the water when it was nearly still, until a soft, pervading female voice from nowhere began repeating in dreamy amplified tones the message: "Passengers on Air Afrique Flight two-zero-nine Paris, Accra, Brazzaville, please report now at gate number forty-three." The voice flowed on into German and French with the same studied softness.

Baako went down to the floor with the DEPARTURES sign and followed the arrows indicating the way to gates 38–45. Next to one set of gates a young African dressed in blue work uniform stood staring a long time at a row of postcards before making up his mind and picking four with the long lean silver lines of the *Concorde* airliner stretched against the unreal blue of a photo artist's sky. A little smile relaxed his lips below the still anxious look in his eyes as he moved toward the counter to pay for this latest dream vision of his life abroad, to be sent to his waiting ones back home.

Now there were small knots of passengers moving along the wide corridor past the series of signs pointing to the gates below. Baako moved with them down a flight of white marble stairs turning in a spiral around a central pillar of new aluminum. On the ground floor the waiting planes could be seen through the glass wall of the final waiting room. An Air Afrique stewardess announced departing time, placed herself at the exit and took the boarding passes extended to her, giving back passports and vaccination certificates. Ahead of Baako, an African in a dark wool suit turned just after he got through the gate, waved and smiled a very happy smile. Baako turned his head, looking behind him to see for whom the smile could have been meant; but all he saw was a line of white faces none of which seemed to have noticed the black man's smile out front. He turned and saw the smiler walking with a confident tread toward the plane opposite.

"Have your passports and vaccination certificates ready, please," repeated the stewardess, "as well as your boarding passes."

Inside the plane, the forward seats seemed all taken, but behind them there were several empty spaces. Baako searched for one next to a window, a little way back of the left wing. He pushed his typewriter into a tight fit on the overhead hand luggage rack. As he did so he noticed four seats in front of him, the generous mass of a wig protruding above the tall back of the seat itself, a shiny black in the gray-white light within the plane. Beside the wig a hand suddenly shot upwards and sideways, its blackness cut off from the blackness of its coat sleeve by a lucent white cuff, and a single finger summoned an advancing stewardess. With a steady smile the stewardess stopped and leaned over listening to the beckoner, and as Baako sat down he saw her shake her head, still smiling while her lips moved making inaudible sounds, and then she said loudly enough, "Later, when the plane takes off." Still smiling, she walked swiftly by, making for the back of the plane. In a moment Baako heard her voice, and then the suppressed titters of the other stewardesses before the red letters shone overhead: NO SMOKING. FASTEN YOUR SEAT BELTS. Simultaneously the amplified sweetness of a caressing female voice flowed softly all through the plane's interior, its smile a very audible part of it.

"*Mesdames et Messieurs*: *Le Commandant Szynkarski et son équipe vous souhaitent la bienvenue à bord de ce DC–8. Nous allons décoller en quelques instants en direction de Brazzaville. Nous ferons escale à Accra . . .*" The voice glided smoothly on into German and then into English. ". . . an oxygen supply is provided for each passenger. Masks are located in the back of the seat in front of you. They can be reached after the panel has been automatically opened."

The plane shook slightly and the noise of engines sucking air rose to a muffled, whining screech, dipped and rose again as the plane rode forward to the edge of the airfield, then turned in a circle with the grass in view to the left. It stopped, but in a few moments the engines were racing again, and this time the crescendo of strength did not fall until the whole craft bumped evenly and rose above the retreating surface below.

The black man in the wool suit made several trips to the rear of the plane and back to his seat, his movements as well as the smile on his face exuding an irrepressible happiness, as if in the atmosphere of the plane he had found an element that suited him completely, and he needed to let everyone and everything around him know this. In his passage every time he bestowed a smile upon Baako, who after the second time looked out through the window and wondered if he could avoid a more direct intrusion from the restless one.

The man in the dark wool suit came over just when the long, thin roads of North Africa were disappearing below and the ripply patterns of Saharan sand, from the blinding yellow into the deep, dark brown, had grown to be all that was to be seen in the distant, endless landscape. He came over with a smile like something learned from the advertisements for beer or whisky or cigarettes made specially for the new Africans, and long moments after he had sat down the smile was still on his face. With careful, studied movements he raised slightly the left lapel of his coat, slid his right hand under it and from somewhere between the coat and the waistcoat produced a packet. The cellophane of it caught the light from the reading lamp just overhead as the man in the wool suit held out the packet.

"Cigarettes?" he offered.

"No. No thanks."

Softly the man in the suit patted his outside pockets. In a moment he had found what he was looking for. He brought out a lighter which seemed to have been sculpted entirely out of light, and gave it a lingering caress just before his thumb brushed smartly across the knob. The flame which shot out was several inches long, but its line was narrow and beautifully controlled, and the man in the suit used it just as it was, waiting till the end of his cigarette had been glowing for seconds already before he began to turn the flame down, slowly, like someone absorbed in deep thought. When the flame died he inserted the lighter back in his pocket.

"You don't smoke?" he asked.

"Sometimes."

The man moved closer, turning in the seat as he did so, and held out his hand.

"Brempong is my name," he said. "Henry Robert Hudson Brempong."

"Baako."

"Is that your Christian or your surname?" Brempong asked.

"No Christian name," said Baako. "I'm not a Christian."

"You know," said Brempong, "you know, your other names." He chuckled, a bit uncertainly, at the end.

"Onipa."

"It's an unusual name," Brempong said.

"My family name," said Baako. "I think of it as a very common name myself."

"Ah, yes," Brempong laughed. "I see what you mean, yes, yes."

Baako saw there would be no way to escape the other's friendly approaches. He took one more look out through his window. Just under the plane he could see a brilliant roll of clouds, and looking at them he felt they were almost tangible, and powerfully inviting. As he stared out the mat of clouds underneath parted once, and through the opening he saw below more of the changing sameness of the Sahara. Over the Mediterranean he had tried, in a way, to produce in himself a mood of complete calm, to ignore every thought, every idea that came to him asking to be followed, to get his mind absolutely free for the understanding of the coming moment. He had wondered what the first sight of the continent would be like for him, and he had watched steadily as the sheet of the blue Mediterranean was left behind.

In the end the actual physical presence of Africa passed under quite softly for him too, like something entirely normal. He had not become suddenly aware of any unusually strong feelings, or indeed of any feeling at all. Instead, it was thoughts that had come to him as the blue sea became brown land, the green of it only an occasional thing against the huge and flowing background. He had had thoughts, very clear and sharp, of the enormity of things here and of the sameness of what was below, and also these strange thoughts, peopled with the living aftermath of amazing crimes still unable to discover what it was that had happened not so very long ago, totally dazed by the present's continuation. And yet, so high above the earth and the water, even thoughts like these had not raised any unusual feelings, or quite simply any feelings at all, except this huge desire for an absorbing quiet.

"I didn't meet you in London," Brempong was saying.

"I haven't been in London," Baako said.

"Ah, that's why, that's why." Then, after a pause, "But where were you?"

"America. New York."

"New York? Oh yes, New York." Brempong hesitated, as if he was sure there was something he wanted to say about New York, something he had forgotten in the passing moment. Finally, apropos of nothing, he said, "It's good to be going home."

Baako smiled, very faintly.

"You are amused," said Brempong.

"Not really." Baako turned slightly, the better to see his fellow traveler. "A little nervous, that's all."

"There's nothing to fear," said his companion, "nothing. Of course at home we can't swing as much as in London, or New York, but . . ."

"That's not what I meant."

Brempong frowned. "I don't get you."

"I don't know what I'm going to find."

"You've been away a long time?"

"Five years."

Brempong smiled expansively. "Do you know how many years, total, I have spent out of Ghana?" Taking a deep puff on his cigarette, he leaned slowly back till his head touched the back of his seat, and then he blew out the smoke in a thin line, directly into the light socket above him. "Do you know? Eight years, total. Eight full years."

"All spent in the same country?"

"Ah, not quite," said Brempong. "And I've been going back home from time to time. But most of the time I was in Britain." He gave a small chuckle. "I know the old country like the back of my hand."

"And you still don't find it hard going back?"

"Oh no. No. But I understand you. I have learned to take precautions, myself. There are important things you can't get to buy at home. Every time I go out I arrange to buy all I need, suits and so on. It's quite simple. I got two good cars on this trip. German cars, from the factory, all fresh. They're following me. Shipped."

Baako looked up, following the curve of the plane's ceiling.

"You see this." Brempong had brought out his lighter. "Where in Ghana would you find a thing like this? Sharp eyes. I bought it in Amsterdam, at the airport, actually. Beautiful things there, Amsterdam. Tape recorders. I took one last year, and it has never given me any trouble." He leaned back completely and his voice relaxed to a quiet sound just above a whisper. "You just have to know what to look for when you get a chance to go abroad. Otherwise you come back empty-handed like a fool, and all the time you spent is a waste, useless." A loud, forced guffaw broke the easy tenor of his voice. "But if you come back prepared, there's nothing to worry about."

"I can't say I am prepared," Baako said. "Not in this way."

"You didn't buy anything to travel back with?"

"Nothing. I was a student."

"Still . . ." the shadow of a smile was playing around Brempong's lips, "you finished your studies."

"June."

"July, August . . . Two months. You're going back in a hurry.

Something urgent?"

"No, not really. After graduation I went to a workshop. It ended last week."

"A workshop?"

"Yes."

"You are . . ." Brempong hesitated, "an engineer . . ."

"A workshop for practicing writers and producers," Baako said.

"Oh yes, oh yes. Yes, yes. Films and things like that." Brempong smiled. "And you are a producer or a writer?"

"I write," said Baako. "Hope to. Try to, anyway."

"So you'll be writing film stories."

"Scripts, yes."

"For Ghanavision Corporation."

"Yes."

"Ghanavision . . ." Brempong stared thoughtfully past Baako out through the window. "Ghanavision. It's not a bad place, actually. You can get ahead very nicely there, very nicely. You know Asante-Smith, don't you?"

"Not personally. Not very well," said Baako. "But I've heard of him."

"Well, he is a young man. Very young, in fact. Not more than five years older than you. How old are you?"

"Twenty-five."

"Well, five or six; seven. Anyway, he's a very young man, this Asante-Smith. But you know already he is the boss of the whole corporation."

Baako laughed softly. "I'm not aiming to become a corporation boss."

"Sure, sure. Not now," said Brempong. "But in a few years, believe me. In a few years." Absently he tried to stub out his cigarette in the small ashtray recessed into the armrest. The attempt was unsuccessful, so that a line of smoke hung over the armrest, faint but steady, only occasionally wavering slightly. The plane took an abrupt drop, but in a moment the flight was smooth again. "Of course," Brempong continued, "a person like Asante-Smith, he knows people. Besides, he is clever. One of his own drinking friends says he has the sweetest tongue in all of Ghana for singing his master's praises. It's the truth. And it doesn't matter to him even when the masters change. He can sing sweetly for anybody who *dey for top*."

Brempong chuckled slowly to himself and, infected, Baako laughed too.

"Some friend," he said.

"That's what I say too," Brempong agreed. "Well, these things are necessary. You have to know people. Big people, not useless people. Top officials who can go anywhere and say 'Do this, do that, for my boy!' "

"You would advise me to hasten to find me a big man, then?" Baako asked.

"Aah, you joke now. You'll soon see. But you have a job already."

"No."

"What?"

"I don't have a job waiting," said Baako. "But first thing I'm going to Ghanavision."

"Mistake," Brempong said with an expression between distaste and exasperated concern. "It's a bad mistake you've made. You've put yourself in a very bad position."

"I don't see what else I could have done. I have my certificates, and if they want to test me . . ."

"It's not like that at all. You don't understand. Look, you don't know those who decide. I know them. If you were an expatriate, a white man, it wouldn't matter. You'd have things easy, even without real qualifications." Brempong let out a long breath. "But when you present yourself with your black face like their own, there's no respect. You'll see."

Baako was quiet for several moments, trying to get an understanding of what the other had said; but in the end, failing to get any real grasp of the words, he let them slide away into the even sound of the plane's flight.

"You didn't see me wave to you — before we came on board."

"I did," Baako answered. "A bit late. And I wasn't really sure it was me you were waving to."

"I wasn't sure either. That you were a fellow Ghanaian. You look different, somehow."

"I never thought I looked so different."

"I don't mean facially. But, you know, how you're dressed, how you walk — you don't give the impression that you know you're a been-to. When a Ghanaian has had a chance to go abroad and is returning home, it's clear from any distance he's a been-to coming back."

"Oh well." Baako heard himself laugh, and the sound was weak and hollow; there was nothing he could do about his embarrassment, nothing he could say to hide it.

"I thought you'd come over and sit with us. My wife would have liked to meet you," Brempong said.

"I wanted a seat by a window. To look out."

"I understand. You don't fly very often."

Baako smiled. A stacked trolley stopped quietly in the aisle to his right and a stewardess leaned over and said softly, "We're serving dinner now. You have a choice of drinks — martinis, white wine . . ." The metalwork of the trolley shone with the softly vibrant light in the plane. Out in front a dark head crowned with the mass of a wig stood suddenly upright. Brempong got up. "I must go," he said. "Eugenia is looking for me." He held out his hand, shook Baako's, and squeezed past the stewardess and the food trolley in the aisle. Baako pressed the blue button at the back of the sat in front of him and disengaged the little folding table. The stewardess placed a tray of ready food on it.

"A ginger ale for me, please."

"One ginger ale, yes," the stewardess echoed, reaching immediately for a squat amber bottle and putting it, freshly opened and fizzing, before Baako. Then she moved on down the aisle.

Baako felt his thirst as a sensation much stonger than his hunger, so that he drank the ginger ale too fast, and then took the paper cup in front of him and drained the water out of it. His body, like some huge, hot sponge, absorbed all that liquid and at the end still had the dry feeling in it, craving more water. He started eating, but after a few mouthfuls he had no appetite left. He tried to eat anyway, but now the taste of meat in his mouth brought back the acid unease that had troubled him so strongly in the morning, the nausea that had pushed him to change his mind so suddenly.

He had thought he would stay a week or so alone in Paris before moving on home, looking, walking around with the little book of street maps and transport line diagrams, getting to see the city and finding out what good films there were to see. But without spending one full day he had fled. He had seen no films, and what he had seen of the city itself before recoiling so abruptly was ridiculously little. It was beautiful, even the small pieces he had seen before the urge to flight became irresistible; but in the attraction of this beauty itself there was the thing that had made enjoyment impossible for him. He had not been able to perceive anything without having it deepen that unsettling feeling that was not only one of loneliness, but a much more fearful emotion, as if there never was going to be any way out of his giddying isolation, a feeling that waiting would only heighten.

The name of the small hotel he had gone to was already lost somewhere in his memory; he saw no point in making the effort to bring it up again. It had been a short walk from there, past cafés in which mirrors doubled the interior space, to the long garden of the Champ de Mars. There was dirt and old paper lying at the bottom of the shallow square ponds there, but the surface was bright with the sun and with the colors of red and white and blue toy boats sailing under little sails or powered by remote control electricity. Above the boats rose the bronze statue of some martial hero trapped in an attitude of triumphant strain. Turning away from it, Baako walked slowly down the wide path to the left of the central lawn. The rust-brown structure of the Eiffel Tower raised in him no curiosity to go up it and see the city from up there. Past pointing cameras and eyes squinting upward and teeth abandoned by the upper lips of upward looking wonderers, he waited for the light to change and then crossed the road running along the river. From the bridge he could see the long flat form of a rusty barge moored on the other bank. In the distance, over the bottom level of the next bridge a stream of cars sped by, each in turn moving ahead of a slow line of subway coaches — two bright green ones in the lead, a red one in the middle, the remaining two a noticeably duller green — passing overhead. Nearer him, on the left bank, a pleasure boat lay idle, with a blue top and the French tricolor drooping behind it, the flapping edge revealing at intervals the painted sign:

THE LAZY DOLPHIN.

Just behind *The Lazy Dolphin* a small khaki-colored military boat bobbed slowly in the algae-green water with three soldiers in battle uniform seated precariously on it sides. Beside them, a girl with a very high, bright yellow miniskirt stood talking, and whatever she was saying made the soldiers laugh incessantly and hold out their arms to her, inviting her to come and fill their patrol boat. But the moment she raised one leg and seemed about to accept, the little boat suddenly shot halfway out of the water and blew away with a violent roar that made the soldiers' laughter no more audible. The boat cut a quick semicircle in the water and then ploughed off in the direction of the double bridge. The girl laughed and waved after her vanishing friends, then turned for the climb up the stairs leading to the street and the bridge above. Halfway up she stopped and sat on a jutting block of concrete bordering the stairway, and, like almost everybody down there now that the soldiers had disappeared in their boat, she stared at a man who had stood facing the quay wall to the left in a frozen attitude of prayer. The man gave no sign that he cared or even knew that he was what all these holiday-makers were looking at. He wore no shoes, and he had taken off his shirt, leaving only a pair of faded blue workers' trousers. He had a dark red skullcap on. Suddenly he broke from his immobile stance and marched directly forward as if it was his intention to march straight through the high wall. But a step or two from it he stopped just as abruptly as he had begun, and raised his arms above his head worshipfully, supplicating the wall. He bowed, took seven steps sideways to the right, three to the left, and sat down finally with his legs in something like the lotus position and his head hanging loosely down. On the bridge, Baako felt drawn by an intense interest in what the man down there was doing in his shut-off world, so that without being really aware of what was happening to him he was beginning to try and understand it all, to enter the closed world. The effort, and the awareness of its futility that came when he looked around him and saw the flow of faces seeking happiness, gave his head a depressing feeling of inner lightness. He turned away, walked across the bridge, across the radiating roads beyond it, making for the fountains of white water where his little map showed a green pattern under the word

TROCADÉRO.

He avoided a girl with fierce, determined eyes, wearing a tight black blouse on top of sausage slacks of green material through which her buttocks were straining for their independence, who came up to him with a Polaroid camera offering to take his picture instantly against the rainbow made by the fountain spray. He climbed some more broad steps and was suddenly in a crowd of children roller-skating intricate patterns all over and around each other. Watching them, he felt a smile ease itself across his face as he saw an old man, his hair white and his remaining teeth yellow and brown with age and tobacco, glide with smooth vigor in an outer circle that enclosed all the children whose presence seemed in no way at all to bother the ancient man. And unlike the children, to whom this skating seemed a serious enough business, the old man was amazingly relaxed, smiling for the benefit of no one but his own self, clasping his hands behind him, placing them on top of his head, or holding them out sideways to steady his glide just when and how the interior spirit moved him. He looked briefly in Baako's direction once as he passed, and Baako looked up and away from him in embarrassment, yet immediately it seemed to him the old man had winked at him in his passage. In their flight Baako's eyes had risen till they came to an inscription high above the crowd below. He would not have read the words if he had not needed to reassure the old skater that he was not staring; but the message up there took his attention, so that he had no need of pretense any more:

TOUT HOMME CRÉE SANS LE SAVOIR
COMME IL RESPIRE
MAIS L'ARTISTE SE SENT CRÉER
SON ACTE ENGAGE TOUT SON ÊTRE
SA PEINE BIEN AIMÉE LE FORTIFIE.

When he climbed up to the central space and crossed over to the other side, he read another inscription on the opposite wall, but could not remember it afterward. The weak feeling was already coming. It was not a feeling of straightforward disgust. There was nothing outside that he had seen to raise in him such a feeling. And within himself what he was aware of was vague: an unpleasant but not at all sharp sensation that everything he had done in about the last half year had been intended as a postponement, a pushing away of things to which he felt necessarily called. On the way back to his hotel he did not go the way he had come, but turned right along the road before the tower, then left along the shaded avenue that bore the sign

AVENUE DE SUFFREN.

Not much traffic passed — a few shiny cars in the soft darkness made by the trees — and he himself overtook a North African alone, pushing little bits of paper in water flowing along the flat gutter with a broom of twigs. When he stepped into the hotel entrance the keeper looked at him and told him he looked ill. He nodded and asked if he could call the airline on the telephone. He was up in his room, lying flat on his back when the call came. He took it.

"*Parlez, monsieur*," the keeper said.

"Invalides?" he asked.

"*Oui, j' écoute*," a woman answered.

"Madame, do you speak English?"

"Yes, I do."

"Good. I'm an Air France stopover passenger. I'd like to change my flight date."

"What is the actual date on your ticket?"

"Next Tuesday."

"You want a change to . . . ?"

"The earliest flight to Accra."

"Today?"

"Is that possible?"

"Yes. But you will have to be quick. There is a flight at sixteen forty-five. Air Afrique. You can take the fifteen-fifteen bus at the Invalides."

"Thank you, madame."

"May I have your name?"

"Oh yes, yes . . ."

★

About an hour after dinner Brempong came back to sit beside Baako. He had been walking up and down the plane with a sort of proprietary familiarity and confidence, obliging stewardesses to squeeze past him, trying available services and asking to buy tax-free tobacco and drinks.

"I like plane travel," he said gratuitously. Baako said nothing. "But it's a pity," Brempong continued, "that you can't take heavy goods in a plane. The nicest things I bought will have to get home by sea. I've insured everything though, but still. You know, for my mother I bought a complete freezer."

"A what?"

"A deep refrigeration plant, commercial model. It ought to be delivered before Christmas. It's a surprise. My mother has always wanted to have a whole bull slaughtered in her yard for Christmas. Now I'll buy the bull and what remains won't decay."

"I see."

'It's no use,' Brempong said, "going back with nothing. You may not have the chance to travel again in a long time. It's a big opportunity, and those at home must benefit from it too. I don't see the sense in returning with nothing. But you haven't had much experience." The voice of a hostess rose softly under Brempong's and finally replaced it: "Ladies and gentlemen, in two minutes we'll be over the oasis of El Oued. Our altitude now is 22,000 feet. Our speed is 682 miles per hour."

Baako looked through the window, searching for the oasis beneath the carpet of clouds. The noise of the engines seemed to swell as he looked downward. When he turned from the window he saw his companion standing up, and out in front there was once more the restless wigged head.

"I must go," Brempong said. Baako leaned forward in a slight bow. When Brempong disappeared down the aisle, he looked down again. The oasis had long since disappeared, and where it was still possible to see the desert its brown expanse was showing fewer and fewer splashes of yellow now. A section of the plane's wing lowered slightly, and an adjacent piece rose just as slightly as the plane made a small turn. Orange dusk sunlight flashed directly into Baako's eyes, then vanished as the plane took a steadier course. Baako let his head lean against the window, but immediately jerked away from the cold contact. He pulled the little curtain of gray and light brown woven tissue across the frozen pane, rested his head upon it, turned out the overhead light and deliberately closed his eyes; but still he felt uncomfortable. His head had not found an angle that could hold it. With his eyes still closed he pressed the armrest lever and let his seat fall back as far as it would go, his head and body falling back with it. Listening in the deepening darkness inside his head, he was able to make out of the noise of the plane's engine patterns that crossed into each other and untangled themselves again — not the undifferentiated whine first heard, but several beats, separate rhythms coming together — and still listening to the sounds he lost awareness of the movement of the machine he was in.

". . . WISH TO INFORM YOU THAT WE WILL BE LANDING IN A FEW MOMENTS AT ACCRA INTERNATIONAL AIRPORT WHERE THE OUTSIDE TEMPERATURE IS 75 DEGREES FAHRENHEIT. WILL YOU PLEASE STRAIGHTEN THE BACKS OF YOUR SEATS, REFRAIN FROM SMOKING AND CHECK THAT YOUR SEAT BELTS ARE PROPERLY FASTENED."

This voice too had the sugary amplified softness, but it had awakened Baako with a feeling of anxiety that would not go away. He tried to relax, staying in his seat and looking out into the darkness below. At first he could see nothing but the night void, but gradually little shaky points of light appeared, turning into weak firefly clusters that became denser every moment. A red light, marking perhaps some high tower, appeared, then after a while a couple of blue lights, and finally the slowly pulsing shaft of strong green light as the plane circled for its descent.

Again Baako waited till the first hurrying people had gone down, then he got up, took his typewriter down and went toward the plane exit. Brempong and his wife were not very far ahead of him. Above the intervening heads he could see the top of the woman's wig, and from time to time the man's back appeared through a momentary gap. At the bottom of the stairs a stewardess asked Baako if he was a transit passenger, and when he said no she took his ticket and tore off a detachable slip from it and said goodbye to him with a lingering smile. He smiled back. Yards away a Ghana Airways bus pulled up and stopped, and the first of the passengers began to climb into it. Baako was surprised to see Brempong raise an arm and wave heroically toward the darkness in front of him before getting into the bus. Only after the bus had brought them to the terminal did Baako understand: behind the lining fence there was a waiting crowd, and several Akan voices had shouted when Brempong's shoes hit the tarmac, "There he comes!" One voice had screamed, "Uncle H.R.H.!" from the darkness, and Brempong had waved once more before he too entered the customs area.

Waiting for his suitcase and his guitar, Baako watched three Ghanaians in suits come in, each holding a sheaf of papers and looking earnestly into the crowd of passengers. One of them relaxed a moment and smiled on seeing Brempong.

"Hello, *Akora*, welcome back," he shouted. "Are your people meeting you?"

"Oh yes, *Akora*, oh yes," Brempong said.

"Good. I have to meet some experts for the Ministry. Expatriates."

"Right ho, *Akora*!"

Brempong's friend moved toward a group of white faces, his teeth already bared in a preparatory welcome smile. The other two made for their own experts.

A tall young man in an open-necked white shirt came in and went directly to Brempong and his wife.

"Ah, there you are, Mensah," Brempong said when he saw him. "They sent you to meet me?"

"Yes sir," the young man said. There were beads of perspiration on his nose. "I'm sorry I'm late, but the police guard wouldn't let me in."

"Why didn't you show him your papers? Didn't they give you any?"

"He was an escort, sir. He asked if I was coming like this to meet a white man. I said no, a Ghanaian. He curled his top lip and just stopped me."

"These escorts are idiots. You should have told him you were meeting a white man."

"I was thinking of that. But a General Police sergeant came and when I showed him the papers he told the escort they were for a very very big man. So I came immediately."

Brempong chuckled and looked at his wife.

"The fools!" the woman said.

"About your luggage, sir," the young man continued, "I have given all necessary instructions. We can go to the arrivals lobby and wait. I think your family is waiting for you there."

"That's right," Brempong laughed happily. "Let's go, Genie." Mrs. Brempong gave most of her gift packages to the young man and the three walked toward the door opposite. Near the door, Brempong wheeled suddenly and called to Baako with perfunctory cheer, "Need any help?"

"No, thanks," Baako said.

His luggage arrived sooner than he had expected, the guitar first, separated from the suitcase by two trunks and a traveling bag. He picked them up and when he came to the customs line the inspector looked briefly into his suitcase, frowned quizzically and asked, "Paper, paper, is that all?"

"That's all," Baako answered, picking up the chalked guitar and suitcase.

A strange scene greeted him as he strode into the arrivals lounge. Three tough-looking men in white jumpers with their cloths balled around their waists were holding Brempong high above their heads. Around them a large crowd of the hero's relatives struggled to get closer to him, shouting, some singing in an ecstatic, emotional confusion.

"Eeeeei! Our white man, we saw you wave! We saw you!"

"The big man has come again."

"Oh, they have made you a white man."

"Complete!"

"And you have come back to us, your own. Thank God."

"Yes, praise him!"

A woman, very fat but still youthful and vigorous, pierced the circle of admirers from outside and shoved her way with demonic energy into the center, shouting with a power that raised her message above the general jubilant cacophony.

"Set him down. Give him to me. Let me embrace him, my precious brother. Hei, hei, let him see his sister, me." The welcomers parted easily before the fat woman's cannonball thrust, their confusion heightening the eye-filling impression of an unending swirl of colored cloth and jewelry. The three men allowed Brempong's feet to touch the floor, and the fat woman bounded onto him in a great leap that threw him back against his stalwart carriers.

"Oooooh my own brother!" she screamed, caught in an orgasmic shudder. "You have come, you have come again to me!"

"Take it easy, Sissie," Brempong said. The fat woman shifted her bulk in a little grotesque dance, her *kente* blouse flapping its elephant-ear sleeves in a whirl of color, her teeth flashing and her blubbery buttocks quivering as she turned and turned in the center around her returning brother. Weeping freely in her joy, looking with insatiate gladness at the traveler just arrived, she wiped her tears and moved with all the crowd out into the night air, shouting, "The champagne! The champagne! Bring the champagne!"

Feeling a steady tension in his groin, Baako asked a policeman on guard if he could look after his luggage, then went through an entrance marked GENTLEMEN. The air inside was uncomfortable with a genital moistness more organic than the sharp smell of urine alone, and he looked up expecting to find the windows shut. They were almost all open. He forced his own urine out in a hurried stream down the yellowed porcelain and quickly emerged out of the fetid air. The policeman gaped in disappointment at him as he thanked him and picked up his luggage and made for the nearest exit. Outside, looking for taxi lights, he walked toward a blinking fluorescent brilliance and found it was no taxi but a large advertising glass box which every few seconds beamed out the message:

> STATE EXPRESS 555
> STATE EXPRESS 555
> STATE EXPRESS 555

When he drew nearer he saw the main sign was not alone. Smaller letters above it flashed the simultaneous exhortation

> Get the taste.

And below the slogan was extended:

> Get the taste
> of international success
> the smooth exquisite flavor
> of a high class cigarette.
> Get the taste.

Nearby the momentary silence was broken by a sudden pop, and the many voices of Brempong's welcoming crowd resumed their excited chatter. The headlights of cars now entering the area once more lit their smiling faces and the riot of blue and green and red and yellow and black and deep gold and purple in the different *kente* cloths out there.

"Give it to me, then!" the fat sister's voice rose again, and the bottle was passed overhead till it reached her in the center. A lone voice gasped audibly, in spite of the spirit of the moment, that this was a lot of expensive drink to waste this way. But the fat sister laughed and shouted, "Kai! Who calls it a waste, that I should bathe

our been-to's feet in the best there is? Kai!" And now Baako saw
Brempong smile and say easily, "Oh, don't worry." The fat sister
leaped with her bulk a few inches in the air, shouting, "You heard
that? Poweeeer! More beyond!" Then she bent down and poured the
drink out over Brempong's shoes while murmurs of approbation
broke out of the admiring circle. Several voices echoed the words
"More beyond!" and the sister laughed a long, abandoned happy
laugh which set the onlooking Baako's ears singing with the
remembered wailing laughter of Afro-Americans beginning a sad
South American carnival song about a hungry dove lost in love.

"Now where's the official car?" a voice asked impatiently.

"Hei, driver, the car!"

"So where has the driver gone now?"

The tall young man who had come to meet Brempong answered
this last question: "He's waiting for us. In the VIP car park." But
this produced an unmollified response.

"Still? Doesn't he know the big man is waiting? Ah, the insolence
of these drivers!"

"Hei driver!" Several claps. "Driveeeeer!"

Baako found himself quite close to Brempong, and the other
recognized him.

"Are you sure you don't need a lift?" Brempong asked him.

"I'm quite all right, really," Baako said. "Thank you."

"Who is that?" the fat sister asked Brempong.

"A friend. I came with him on the plane."

"You mean he is also a been-to?" she asked, inspecting Baako
with suspicious thoroughness, from head to toe. "I must say he
doesn't . . ."

"By the way," Brempong said quickly, cutting the fat one short,
"let me give you my card." He took out a wallet from his inside
breast pocket and extracted a card from it. The leather was green,
embroidered with a gold leaf pattern that seemed to resolve itself
into a monogram in the flash of the cigarette ad light. Baako took the
card.

"Moroccan," Brempong smiled as he closed his wallet carefully
and inserted it back in his pocket.

The long shape of a limousine detached itself from the row of
guarded vehicles parked deep beyond the ordinary cars, its turning
headlights catching the luminous letters of the sign at the special
entrance:

V.I.P. CAR PARK
NO ENTRY
By order

As the big black car slowed to a purring stop, Brempong's welcomers started a soft stampede to get to it, but the fat woman stopped it.

"Move back, you villagers," she said, pushing hard against those in her way. "Don't come and kill him with your TB. He has just returned, and if you don't know, let me tell you. The air where he has been is pure, not like ours. Give him space. Let him breathe!" She pushed till she had created some space around the hero. An old woman ventured into the space and began to ask a question: "But how shall we . . ." But the fat woman drove her back into the crowd, then whirled around, stripping off her large *kente* stole in a movement of unexpected swiftness. She laid the glittering cloth on the asphalt leading to the back door of the limousine and called out, "Come, my been-to; come, my brother. Walk on the best. Wipe your feet on it. Yes it's *kente*, and it's yours to tread on. Big man, come!"

Brempong let her lead him over the rich cloth, nodding and smiling as she yelled repeatedly to him, "Stamp on it, yes, great man, walk!"

Apart from the fat woman, two more people, a man and a woman, both in *kente*, got in the back with Brempong. The tall young man shut the door after them and got in front beside the driver. The old woman who had been pushed out of the way passed in front of Baako, muttering, "Ei, ei! This is some disease that has descended upon us. My last cedi, and I must spend it at this time, because I was mad enough to agree to come and welcome someone's swollen peacock." Behind her the car horn gave a sudden violent blast. She staggered sideways, and inches beside her, like a slow, fat worm the car slid past toward the road out. The light inside it was on, and it seemed to Baako as if the back of it was filled entirely with color, laughter, teeth and light. Just as it turned left onto the road, the big band brake lights went on behind it, and its number plate shone clearly:

Baako followed the beaten old woman, catching up with her before she reached the taxi ranks. He was thinking of what to say to her when she spoke first.

"*Owura*," she said. "I am going to Adabraka. Asylum Down. If you are going that way, perhaps it will not be hard if I come with you?"

"I think I will go the same way."

"I thank you very much, *Owura*. You have saved me."

One taxi driver put out his roof light when Baako approached and said, "No, I'm waiting for someone in there." A second switched off his light and slowly rolled up his window, saying nothing at all. The third man Baako came to got out and came toward him.

"Taxi?"

"Yes."

The driver put the suitcase in the taxi trunk while Baako let the old woman in and sat beside her in the back. In a moment the on-off glow of the big cigarette advertisement had disappeared behind the accelerating car. A few yards from the junction with the main road into town a sign held overhead on thick white pillars proclaimed:

WELLCOME!

At the junction itself, while the driver waited for three slow incoming cars to pass, Baako read the words of a smaller sign saying goodbye to departing travelers about to use the Ghana International Airport. The ride in was smooth, and the brightness of the main road lighting had about it an element of newness that was heightened as the taxi got nearer the center. Large, new buildings slid unhurriedly by. Baako asked the driver what they were and in answer got a small flow of strangly casual answers: "That one? Trade Union Congress. Labor Office. Farmers' Secretariat. Tax."

"They are all lit."

"Sure. Every night," the taxi driver said.

"Why?"

"Why not?" The driver chuckled. "Show beez. Is beautiful, not so?"

"You think so?"

The driver shrugged and did not answer.

Baako felt something else rising in him to add itself to that feeling of isolation and unease from which he had thought he was fleeing. He found it very hard trying to force the feeling into thought that he could grasp, and yet it was there, like a very strong pulse that gained in the potency of its beat with the awareness of every new event and every new thing that had passed outside. His own departure was far away and hazy in his memory now, except for an overriding sense that too much of it had been a matter of the outward show. He was unsure now why there was in him this dread of his being somehow forced into a repetition of things with no meaning for his own life, until he thought again of Brempong and the family that had come so lovingly to welcome him. A sharp pain pricked his left temple. He winced and did not open his eyes. Laying his head far back on the seat, he saw the darkness inside his head filling with the sweating, smiling, suited figure of Brempong, caught happily in the center of his crowd like a man who had looked forward so long to just some such beautiful sort of trap. For a moment he thought perhaps they all knew, Brempong and the crowd, that what they had just done would be a brief ceremony, to be forgotten so that the returned traveler could return to life in a way that would not make it all a long continuation of a desperate inflated game that had forcibly to stay different, much larger than any possible real life here could be. It was not just in his frightened imagination. He had seen this first thing: an invitation into a pretended world, happily given, happily taken, so completely accepted that there had hardly been any of the pretenders to whom it could have seemed unreal. What power would Brempong find to sustain such a dizzy game? Or perhaps he had found as much of this power as was necessary. After all, the crowd around him had been just as willing to raise him skyward as he had been willing to let himself be lifted. Perhaps he was not likely to be worried about the power needed for this game, because like all the eager ones around him he had found in the game itself an easy potency he had not had to struggle for, to create. In spite of himself, Baako found a kind of fearful wonder invading him. A man had gone away, spent time elswhere, grown months and years, and then returned. Those he had left behind had spent time too, grown along their different waves, waiting to welcome their traveler. In the end they had come waiting for him with a ceremony in their hearts, and amazingly it had happened that whatever strange ceremony he had been rehearsing inside his own being had been a perfect answer to theirs. Amazing, since these had been no mere laid-down ceremonies, but things growing with an obvious, wild freedom right here and now. Now Baako could feel his own fear more sharply. It was not something he could explain, not now. But there was in his flight something of an impotent resentment whose absence accounted for at least a large part of Brempong's happy world. It was not just the feeling that he would be destroyed in it, explode from something within; even if he had felt like it, he was sure there was a wall between him and Brempong. Maybe the man could see something he was blind to, or maybe he had eyes denied the exhilarated Brempong. At any rate, he would need to be the careful one.

It was not a mere game. Not to the welcomers he had seen this night. More insistently, Baako saw the ceremony working itself out: the straining crowd, the clothes, the jewels, the cascading drink, the worship of this new chief, the car, the words in the night. Did it matter whether there was real power or real joy as long as the human beings involved thought there was? So what if these words and ceremonies were the mere outward show of power and joy hiding impotence? Who was going to stand outside it all and say maybe the show was designed to hide impotence, but all it did was steep this powerlessness in a worsening stupidity? And who would stop laughing and praise-singing long enough to hear such words?

"*Owura*," a distant voice said. Baako opened his eyes.

"*Owura krakye*," the old woman next to him was saying, with a voice diminished as if in awe, "if it pleases you, we are approaching the neighborhood where I live."

"Oh, just tell the driver when we're there," Baako said.

The taxi had turned off the bright main road and was going much more slowly now.

"There, at the Cathedral roundabout, after the crazehouse," the old woman said, pointing ahead.

The driver stopped immediately after the circle, let the old woman out and moved off again before she had finished saying her long thanks.

"Where are we going?" the driver asked. "Where is your home?"

"I was just thinking . . ." Baako said. "Are there any hotels around now?"

"The new ones are behind us. Star, Continental, Ambassador. But in this area there are the same old ones. Avenida, Ringway. They say the Avenida is fine." The driver idled his machine. "I thought you had a home in this town. Or don't you know anybody? A friend?"

"Oh, I don't think you'll know any of my friends."

"Try. Man never knows."

"O.K. Do you know where Fifi Williams lives?"

The driver laughed loud and long. "Never say die!"

"Why, do you know?"

"No. But everybody knows him. Ghana Bank, not so?"

"Yes."

"Young been-to. He must be at the Star now. He's a real guy. Swinging nigger."

"A what?"

"Swinging nigger. You don't know the latest terms here," the taxi driver said. "Swinging nigger. That means a tough guy. Plenty of good time."

"I see."

"No, I don't know his bungalow," the driver repeated, still coasting.

"Let's go to the Avenida, then."

"Fine."

The car picked up speed, its lights making the low gutter culverts flash yellow as it left intersections behind, then turned left and followed the slow curve of a gravel drive and stopped before the Avenida Hotel.

"Eighty pesewas," the driver said after he had put the suitcase on the hotel veranda.

"Will you take a dollar? I haven't changed my money."

"Sure."

The taxi drove off over the gravel and back out onto the road outside, its back fenders a dark orange color in the red glow of the tail lights. In the small hotel lobby also the light was a shaded amber, and the clerk behind the polished mahogany table looked more than half asleep. He told Baako the only rooms left were in the annex, and when Baako nodded he filled out a form and asked him to pay the price in advance.

"I have only travelers' checks," Baako said.

"They're all right."

"How much?"

"Nine cedis. Nine dollars," the clerk said, not looking up.

Baako signed a ten-dollar travelers' check and the clerk gave him back a note that had a dark turquoise color.

"One new cedi," he said with a tired sigh, rising and coming round his table. "Follow me. We'll go to the annex."

Baako followed the clerk down the driveway, across the road, down a small side street and then right along a wide, sandy alley. At their approach a lean dog began howling like a frightened beast and hopped off on three legs, making for deeper shadow. It continued its howling as the clerk stopped in front of a big two-story building, opened the gate and said, "Here." He led the way up the cement stairs, raising the suitcase above his head till he came to the top, went straight along an unlit corridor almost to the end and stopped before an unmarked door. He opened it and switched on a lamp beside a low bed.

"The bathroom and lavatory are here," he said as he walked out, pointing with his thumb. "Breakfast is at eight, in the main hotel dining room."

"Thank you," Baako said.

When the clerk's steps were no longer audible Baako lay on his back upon the bed, looking at the bare ceiling. Occasionally the muffled sound of a motor passing along the road outside rose softly and died down, like a sea wave. The air inside smelled humid and stale. Baako got up and went to the window. An air-conditioner was fixed directly under it, but it was not working. He opened the window as far as it would go, but he did not feel any immediate inrush of air. Instead, the howling noises made by the dog rose again, stopped briefly and continued. He went out to the end of the corridor, trying to make up his mind about a shower. But inside the bathroom the light socket had no bulb in it, and he came back and sat on the bed. Now he felt an ambiguous comfort, savoring this sense of being so alone back home, connected for the moment to no one, with no one save himself knowing where he was. Wondering why he did not have more of a feeling of being lost, he took off his clothes and left them on the chair and table beside the bed. Going back to the bed, he stopped, opened the guitar case and took out the instrument. The student from whom he had bought it had talked a long time to him when he had gone to get it, starting with the information that he wouldn't always need a tuning fork: he could pick up a telephone and listen to the dial tone, and it would give him an exact B flat sound, a fret down on the fifth string. His Parthian shot had been to tell Baako that his wanting a guitar meant he had begun to run from human beings. "That thing is going to be your companion, all you need," he said, scratching his thin neck. "It even has a female shape, a bit stylized I admit, plus a goddam hole big enought for the mythical African prick." And then the fellow had counted the money Baako paid him very carefully to make sure he was not being cheated.

His left fingers curved and placed themselves automatically for an E chord, but before he could begin picking, the theatricality of all these gestures he had made came nauseatingly to him, and he rose to put the guitar away and got into the bed. There was no second sheet, but he did not find the feel of the blanket irritating. He was thinking and wondering whether there were any people here who had escaped the roles held out to them by the powerless hopers close to them. He would have to be careful. Unless those near him could want him not playing roles, but as his own changing self: impotent sometimes, growing, sometimes strong, confused, often weak, changing, many things by turns.

Under him the sheet felt moist, but between it and the covering blanket there was warmth. Outside, the dog raised its voice in an unbelievably long howl which did not stop but became a yelping sound and then a whimper growing always fainter as the dog and the sky seen through the window and the sound of passing cars dissolved into the wider quietness around.

*

In the morning he woke up and went immediately to the bathroom. There was a soft diffused light entering through a side window, and for his shower he found a small cake of green soap and a white towel, old and very dry in a stringy way. He walked over to the main hotel building and found the night clerk's place behind the mahogany table taken by a young girl with violet lips and a wig of light brown hair. Behind her a small wall clock indicated it was twenty past ten. The girl was in the middle of a telephone conversation.

"I came last night," Baako told her. "What time do I have to move out?"

The girl let a slow laugh end itself before she covered the mouthpiece and said with obvious irritation, "Twelve." Her side of the conversation seemed to consist entirely of laughter and gentle ejaculations that could have meant either surprise, admiration or both.

"I'd like to make a call after you," Baako cut in, and waited. She seemed not so much to be ignoring him now as to have completely lost all awareness of his presence. When the time read ten-thirty, Baako walked out to the road again and stopped the first taxi he saw.

"Ghana Bank," he said.

"High Street?" the driver asked.

"Is that the central office?"

"The biggest."

"Good," Baako said. "That should be it."

The ride was short. The driver gave Baako two large coins in exchange for the dollar he gave him and let him out. To his right he saw a small, shaded space overflowing with tough-looking children carrying crates of colored Biro pens and fighting over the few buyers there, and women in a crooked row selling identical lots of fruit and cakes and bread, then beggars sprawled haphazardly in what spaces they could find in the press. The Bank was to the left, on the other side of a large car park. Sunlight shot sharply back off rows of parked cars that seemed all new and freshly polished, and beyond them it bathed the gold-leaf grille of the building's facade in a surfeit of brightness. At intervals along the shiny cagework medallions bore all the ancient symbols in sculpted relief: twin pods of cocoa, sets of Ashanti gold weights, the complete line of spokesmen's staffs for the seven Akan clans, the swords of the old royal executioners crossed ceremonially, stools, elephants and palm trees, a heavy fold of *kente*, *akwaaba* dolls with their mocking, innocent faces, and above all the repeated figure of the protean spider Ananse, always in a different position along the turns and the radiating lines of his web.

A young clerk in a white shirt and striped blue tie took him to a side entrance, up two flights in a lift so new it still smelled of paint and cement, and stepped out to show him the way along a shaded corridor.

"His door is Number Three," he said.

"Thank you."

A loud, hearty voice answered when he knocked, and he went in. For a small moment Baako was not sure. The sound of an air conditioner reached him simultaneously with the blast of cold air. There was a man behind the big desk opposite him, talking relaxedly to a woman whose back and wig were the only things visible to Baako at first. The man got up, and Baako relaxed. He did not really look entirely like Brempong.

"Christ almighty . . . Baako!"

"Hi, Fifi," Baako said, shaking hands.

"Ei, Baako!" Fifi shouted. "When did you come?"

"Last night."

"But why, man, why didn't you let me know? Your mother said you would stay in Europe a bit and come next month."

"I changed my mind."

"Ei, Baako. You're now an American," Fifi said, looking at him from head to toe. "A thin American." The woman laughed, and Fifi turned abruptly to her: "Oh, look, Christina, pardon me, but this is Aunt Efua's son, Baako."

"The one who was in America?" the woman asked. A smile spread upward from her lips, animating her eyes.

"Aunt Efua has only one son," Fifi said, laughing.

"Oh Feef," she protested with a tired, feminine languor, "you're such a bad man." Then she held out a small hand and in the same tone said to Baako, "Welcome home, been-to stranger."

The woman had an unmistakably seductive air about her. When she spoke, she drew the words out as if she herself were deep inside a dream from which she was relucant to emerge, so that every syllable fell from her lips with the softness of something lubricated with a sensuous and delicious fatigue. No movement of hers was quick. Even the closing and opening of her eyelids was done as if any normal speed would cancel the pleasure she got from them.

"Have you seen your mother yet?" Fifi asked.

"No," Baako said. "You know, I don't know where she lives now."

"You don't know her house number?" Fifi asked, absently; then he added: "What am I talking about. They haven't numbered the houses in Accra yet. Not properly."

"But they will soon," Christina said, "in the year two thousand *kojo* ten." She sighed a long sigh. "Well, Feef, I have to go now."

"When can I see you again?" Fifi asked her.

Christina chuckled lazily. "You know it depends on you," she sang deliberately, eyes closed, "and your holy wife who won't let you come and play . . . and your beautiful car which she wants to monopolize . . . and your money which she wants for herself alone, and your sweet *kojo* magic which she can't share at all. But as for me, Feef, I'm ready any time."

"Saturday?"

"I'll believe you when I see your handsome face, Feef."

"We can meet at the Star."

"And don't forget . . ."

"I'll let you have it, I promise."

"A promise is a promise is a promise is a promise," she said, getting up to go. The air around her was softly filled with a sweet suspicion of powder and sweat, perfume and sex. "Oh, by the way," she said at the door, "if you can't escape, send the new been-to to see me. I hope he brought his car." The door closed behind her.

"Who is she?" Baako asked.

"Christina . . ." Fifi laughed uneasily, "just one of the girls."

"Man," Baako said softly, laughing back.

"There'll be dozens like her after you the moment they smell you out. You heard her saying it; the new been-to."

"They'll run backward then when they see I have no car."

Fifi's eyes narrowed in surprise. "It's coming by sea?"

"What's coming?" Baako asked.

"Your car," Fifi answered in a patient tone.

"I haven't got one."

"I see." Fifi looked embarrassed. He hummed a nonsensical snatch and motioned to Baako to sit in the chair left by the woman Christina. "Let me try and get your mother on the phone."

The call took some time. It seemed it was not a simple affair, but that the receptionist had to be joked with and promised things before she finally agreed to make the connection for the laughing Fifi.

"Hello, hello, hello? May I speak to Mrs. Onipa? Ah, Aunt Efua, I have a huge present waiting here for you . . . No . . . No . . . No, it speaks and breathes . . . Oh no hahahaha . . . No . . . No, I'll tel you . . .

No, hohohohoho Aunt Efua, you're as bad as I am now. Look, take a deep breath and close your eyes . . . That's right. Now count . . . Ready? Baako is here . . . Now . . . In this office . . . I swear . . . Would I joke with something like this? I'm serious. You can speak to him. All right, I agree . . . And if I'm right, what will you give me? Agreed . . . Agreed. Don't go anywhere. Bye." Fifi sighed and shook his head, putting back the handset. "She's afraid I'm joking. Her voice was shaking, I don't blame her. But why didn't you send her a cable, Baako, why? You're so strange."

Down in the car park an old guard opened the door for Fifi and maintained a humble half-crouch till he got in and pulled it shut. Baako went round the front of the car to the other side. It was a white Mustang, its glittering chrome racehorse symbol bent with compact power and speed and shimmering in the sun as Baako passed it. Fifi drove to the hotel first to pick up the luggage, then sped with confident ease through the center of the town and came to a stop before a large, luridly painted sign:

RADIANTWAY INTERNATIONAL DAY NURSERY.

There was an accompanying picture, a crude thing in clear colors, of a little boy and girl, both African but very light-skinned, standing facing a long flight of steps topped by a brilliant rising sun.

> *A bright start now*
> *To a successful future.*
> Write to The Head Teacher,
> Radiantway,
> P.O. Box 0712,
> Accra.

"Here we are," Fifi said. He led the way across the open gutter into an office facing the street. From somewhere in the yard within came the high voices of children singing in unison:

> Jaaack and Jill
> Went aaap the hill
> To fetch a pail of waaatah . . .

"Ah, Mr. Williams," said a gray-haired man, rising from his desk, "glad to see you here. Is it one of your little relatives . . .?"

"No, Principal," Fifi said, and Baako saw the old man smile a smile full of pleasure at the mention of the title, "not this time. I rang Mrs. Onipa about half an hour ago. She's expecting me."

"Oh yes," the old man said. "One moment, Mr. Williams." He walked toward an open door in the back leading to the yard.

There was a sharp rap on the door before the old man reached it and then Baako saw his mother. She had entered quietly, almost timidly, but the moment she saw him it seemed as if some potent force had filled her and made her forget all else around; she gave him no time to move — with a soundless leap she threw herself against him, and he felt her whole body quivering as he too held her close, her head slightly bowed and resting against his chest. Then she pulled away a pace and stared upward into his eyes. Her eyes were wet and red now, and when she began to speak her emotion made her lips work against her words, so that she had to stop after nearly every word.

"Oh, Baako," she said, trying to smile through her tears, "you came so suddenly. You didn't give us time to get ready for you."

"It's all right, Efua," Baako said. "I changed my plans."

"Aaaaaahaaa," the old man was nodding, "this is the son, then?"

Baako saw his mother's face as she tried without success to frame more words before collapsing once more against him, trembling and sobbing. It was Fifi who spoke to the gray-haired man. "Principal, I forgot to make the introduction. This is Baako." Baako shook hands and the old man said, "Pleased to meet you," before turning to his mother with a broad smile. "It's a blessed day for you, Mrs. Onipa. Take the afternoon off to give him a fitting welcome."

"Thank you, Principal, thank you," she said.

He caught his mother's face from time to time when he looked in Fifi's rearview mirror and saw her sitting in one corner of the back seat. She was smiling now, completely at ease in the enfolding luxury of the red leather upholstery. Once she tried suddenly to wave to some vanishing person along the way, and when she steadied herself again she had a smile of joy and final triumph on her lips. In a moment she was leaning forward all the way to touch his left ear and cheek, and she was asking in a near-whisper filled with wonder and gladness, "When is yours coming, Baako?"

"What?" he asked, surprised.

"Yours, your car, so that my old bones can also rest." But before Baako could find an answer Fifi had raced his engine to a noisy stop and was saying in a too joyful voice, "Auntie, we're home!"

4 : Awo

IT WAS A SUDDEN CRY, long and full of fear, followed by the feeble plop of a soft fall. There was no one else in the house at this time in the morning, save Araba and Naana. Quickly, he took a shirt off a peg behind the door and rushed out across the central hall. But his grandmother was ahead of him, just on the point of turning the corner towards Araba's room, though she was walking at her usual slow, blind pace. She heard him coming and, as if she had felt a need to explain her own uncanny speed, turned to him and said, "Blood, Baako, I smelled blood."

"Go back, Naana," he said, holding her arm. "Go back to your room and rest. I will go and see what made Araba cry out."

"It is the baby; I smelled blood," Naana said, her eyes staring and her closed mouth trembling with her fear. "But, Great Friend, this is such an early time for him to come, if he is to stay now."

"Go back, Naana. I will take care of her."

"I know," the old woman said, trying to smile, and turned to go back into her room. He moved swiftly past the two little storerooms to his left, along the narrow passageway.

The door to Araba's room was wide open, but from the outside only the foot of the double bed within was visible, together with the carefully arranged pyramid of trunks and suitcases, each covered with a separate pink coverlet edged with blue and yellow embroidery. The window was half shut, so that it took Baako a few moments after he had entered to see clearly what had happened. Araba was sitting in an exhausted position, her back leaning against the side of the bed and her legs spread apart in front of her. She was staring up and straight ahead, and when Baako entered she did not seem to have enough energy to turn her head and look at him. There was blood on the uneven cement floor underneath her, filling a small hollow and beginning to flow over in a small stream running between her thighs. Apart from the blood, there was nothing else.

"Relax, Araba," Baako said. Holding her around the back with his left, he slipped his right arm under her thighs and lifted her off the floor and onto the bed. She held his left wrist in a strong grip, and her eyes now had in them the uncertain look of panic.

"Relax," he said again. "I must go out and get a taxi, and we'll go to the hospital."

"Call Kwesi," she said weakly.

"Later," he answered. "Tema is a long way, and we have to get to the hospital first. Don't worry, I'll be with you." She smiled a little, but still kept hold of him, so that he had to disengage himself gently and reassure her again before going out.

He ran out into the yard, past the gate, turning right as he came to the street. He kept running till he reached the Link Road junction with the street. In several minutes only one car passed that way, a gray Mercedes with some plump-cheeked official in the back of it. He ran faster, all the way down to the Kaneshie market, to the big junction made by the Winneba and Link roads. An empty taxi appeared, slowing down as Baako raised his right hand. But just as the driver was about to come to a complete stop, his face took on a horrified look and he swerved sharply back into the stream of traffic on the left and was off. For one moment Baako wondered what could have been the matter; then he raised his hand to flag down a second coming taxi and he smiled: his right hand was smeared with blood. He let it fall to his side and used his left instead. The second taxi stopped very close to him. The driver gave two happy, relaxed toots on the horn.

"Get in, brother. Anywhere in Ghana, ready to go!" he said, turning to look at his passenger.

"First we go up Link Road, toward the little power substation."

"Yeaaah, Jack, I'm with you."

"After that we turn left. I'll point out the way."

"Finety!" the driver said. He made a sharp U turn and raced up the Link Road hill. He had a car radio, turned on not too loud, so that he could sing along with the bands as they played their high life tunes. He had a good clear voice, and he plainly enjoyed singing the words, as if all of them had in some way come out of himself and the life he led.

So many days I ask myself

the sum of this my life
what will it be?
Ninety tangled threads I have
~~to unravel to make this my life~~
and all I have to help me
is the darkness about me, ahhhh.

"We go left here," Baako said.

"Goodoh!" the driver said with enthusiasm, but almost immediately he slammed on his brakes and looked back at Baako. His eyes were glued to the bloody right hand.

"Hey, man, what is this? Did you kill a human being?"

"No," Baako answered. "It's my sister. She's ill — a baby coming."

"Aaah oooh, I see," the driver said. "I'll be quick, then." The car shot forward and came to a springy stop before the yard gate.

"Could you come and help me? She's inside."

"Oh sure." The driver stepped out and banged his door shut. "Don't close your side." The two entered the yard and the house, the driver whistling softly all the time. From Naana's room her voice came, disturbed and timid: "That is you, Baako, but who is the other?"

"A friend, Naana. Don't worry."

"If he is a helper, that is good."

"You took so long, Baako," Araba said. "I was afraid."

"Everything will be all right. I found a taxi." He took Araba in his arms, feeling her wet cloth under her, while the driver kept her head from falling back. They put her across the back seat of the taxi, and Baako sat in front with the driver, reaching back to hold her hand all the way to the hospital. The driver drove fast, and once he cut in across moving traffic so closely that Baako held his breath.

"Don't worry," the driver said. "I started driving when I was seventeen. Ten years, no accident. A baby, that's more serious than the police. Let them arrest me now. I'll ask them if they know the way inside their mothers — where they came from. No fear. A baby is number one." The dry gray expanse of salt flats left behind by the Korle Lagoon slipped rapidly by behind occasional mounds of greenery, and the driver passed every other vehicle. His radio was still on, and when a song pleased him he broke into it.

Some were born so low
flat down on their backs
so cool night and bright morning
they can see their god
up there in his sky.
Some were born on stilts
placed on strong rooftops
so where do you find the wonder
that they don't take so long
to look tall in this life?

The driver whistled with the guitar solo where it took over, and in places he even slipped in an extra wry note of his own. He took the turning to the hospital so sharply that his brakes shrieked, but in the back Araba was very quiet.

"This is the new maternity ward," the driver said when he came to a stop in front of a tall new concrete and glass structure. He called out to a passing nurse, "*Awuraa* Nurse," and the nurse came closer, squinting with ill humor, "there's a baby being born in this car."

"Are you the father?" the nurse asked, looking at Baako.

"No." He pointed to Araba in the back. "She's my sister."

"Are you a Senior Officer?"

"Look, I'm not in the Civil Service yet."

"Well," the nurse could hardly contain her disdain, "is the real husband a Senior Officer?"

"No," Baako said. "But why are you asking?"

"Look, beautiful *awuraa* Nurse," the driver said, winking broadly at the girl, "the woman is suffering."

"Taxi driver!" The nurse made the words come out like shots. "I am not speaking to you." The driver looked away and whistled the refrain of the last high life song he had been singing. "So what is your status?" she asked, turning to Baako again.

"I have no status," he said. He saw the nurse's brows rise and the corner of her lips fall.

"Well," she said. "This new wing is for VIP's and Senior Officers. The rest, to the old wards."

"And where are the old wards?"

"There!" The nurse pointed with perfunctory disdain, and swung off into the interior of the modern building.

"Ghana life sweet oh!" the driver shouted after the disappearing nurse. Then he turned to Baako and said reassuringly, "I know the old wards. Many times I took people there." He turned the car round and after a short ride he stopped in front of a ward where even from the outside Baako could see the mosquito gauze had turned green and the paint on the wood holding it had come off. "This place for broke people." The driver smiled.

"Araba," Baako said, "I'm going in to find a nurse. Everything will be all right. Wait for me." He smiled at her, but she did not make even the shadow of an attempt to smile. The look of panic that had been in her face had disappeared. Now all he could see was a flat, hurt look. Her lips moved once, but he heard nothing distinct except something that sounded like *been-to*. He walked into the ward.

He found a nursing sister in blue uniform who walked briskly out with him when he told her his sister was bleeding; on the way out she shouted several times, "Issa, Issa, bring a wheelchair, quick!" Moments after they got to the taxi a bony man in khaki shorts and shirt with Frafra marks on his face joined them, pushing a dark green invalid's chair before him. The three men lifted Araba onto it and the one called Issa wheeled her into the ward.

"She's lost a lot of blood," the nurse said. "We'll be giving her a transfusion. Can you give blood? Our bank is very low."

"Yes," Baako answered. "Right now?"

"In a minute. I'll be where you found me."

The back seat of the taxi was wet with blood, but when Baako apologized, the driver shook his head. "Brother, it's only the blood of a new human being. Luck to you, luck to me." He took his fare and was visibly surprised when Baako gave him an extra cedi; then he recovered quickly and said thanks, adding, "You see, my luck is in already."

The blue nurse was fast and efficient. She had Baako wash his hands of Araba's blood and she herself supervised the taking of his blood before letting him go to the section where Araba had been taken.

"It's not visiting time, you know," she said without a smile, "but this is an emergency. Don't stay too long."

It was past eleven when he left the hospital. He walked down to the new VIP maternity wing, then turned along the road leading into town, looking for a bus. At the stop he did not go directly to take his place in the line of waiting people, but moved over to the large Municipal Transport Authority sign on which the official bus timetable had been printed. The sign indicated there would be a bus every seventh minute. When he went back to join the line the woman just ahead of him turned and smiled at him.

"You went to read the sign," she said, as if that statement itself carried a well-known message.

"Yes," he answered. The woman laughed. Half an hour later, when Baako left the queue to stop a taxi, the woman laughed again and asked him for a ride.

"Civil Service Commission," he told the driver.

"One cedi flat," the driver answered sullenly. The woman gaped, but said nothing.

"O.K. But hurry," Baako said. "I'm late."

*

The Junior Assistant to the Secretary of the Civil Service Commission sounded furious.

"Your're very late. The appointment was for eleven."

"I had to take my sister to the hospital," Baako said. "She almost had a miscarriage."

"You'd better know I'm a busy man," said the Junior Assistant, picking his teeth with a dry nib. "A very busy man. I can't waste time like this." With great concentration he stuck the nib into a blotting pad in front of him, and when he extracted it the soft deposit from between his teeth was left on the pad. "You will have to come tomorrow."

"This is the fifth time you're telling me that."

"Come tomorrow."

"Look, all I want to know is what's happening to the papers I filled out."

"I said come tomorrow." The Junior Assistant raised his brows in irritated contempt, but his eyes remained practically closed.

"This isn't serious," Baako said.

The Junior Assistant to the Secretary of the Civil Service Commission gave his head a slight upward tilt. "You want to be serious with me?"

"I want to know what's happening to my papers."

"You want me to help you?"

"I'm not asking you for help. I filled the forms . . ."

"Ah, weeeell." the Junior Assistant rose, shrugging. "You understand me. You can come and see me when you decide you want me to help you. And don't come here just to waste my time. I'm a busy man. I have my post." He left the office. Minutes went by and he had not come back. It was when Baako walked out into the sun and the dust of the official car park outside that he saw the Junior Assistant to the Secretary of the Civil Service Commission standing in the shade of a nim tree, smoking and chatting contentedly with one of his colleagues. Crossing the main road, Baako walked in the shadow of the trees lining it, the sound of sea waves coming clearly to him from the right, till he came to the huge roundabout at the arch, where he stopped another taxi.

"Where?" the driver asked as he came to a stop.

"Achimota."

"One fifty."

"O.K."

★

"No, but truly, Onipa, not many of you come back to see me. And call me Kofi. No master nonsense now. You're taller than I am now, and the baby face now has a beard, God save us. Now just give me a mo, and I'll finish this head. I have to be careful."

Baako walked around the large studio while his old art master finished his terra-cotta head. There were no desks now, and the easels were fewer; but the walls were lined with rows of black heads in dozens of different attitudes from sweet repose to extreme agony. They had been arranged in some kind of rough order, so that the tension captured in the heads seemed progressively to grow less and less bearable, till near the end of the whole series, when Baako had almost arrived back at the beginning, the inward torture actually broke the outer form of the human face, and the result, when Baako looked closer, was not any new work of his master but the old, anonymous sculpture of Africa. One painting drew his attention; it was unfixed, just lying there, a crucifixion tableau with the crosses shown a rough texture and the man in the middle a very small young man, tanned black under a pitiless sun. It bore the signature: Kofi Ocran '61.

"Secretly," the artist was now saying, "I had hoped you would become an artist, Onipa. I'm glad I didn't force the idea on you, though. It might have turned you completely against creative work."

Ocran locked the studio door and the two walked down the road to his bungalow. Behind them a bell rang faintly and then a confused murmur of voices came from the dining hall as the students spilled out after lunch. Baako looked back just once, and the sight of uniformed students filled him with a feeling that was not nostalgia at all, but a semblance of panic, as if time could absorb him into itself and drive him along the edge of some endless, vertiginous cycle over and over again. Ocran walked not on the tarred surface of the road but on the brown laterite beyond the little open drain alongside it, touching the rough barks of the mango trees lining the road, and stopping once to watch a knot of red ants climbing up one of the trees.

"I don't understand it," Ocran continued. "I've had six, maybe seven students pass through my hands who really had something, and I hoped they would want to do good work. Artistic work, with clay, ebony, paint, with textures, shaping things to say what is inside themselves. You were one. But the best, I've never been able to make them understand. You all go off to do Physics and Medicine and that stupid Law and things like that. I've never succeeded in understanding that."

"You don't consider writing creative, then?"

"Words," Ocran said with a light shrug. "Words. No. Too many words are just lies. You can't fool anyone with things that have texture. You really have to create. Too many words are just used for telling lies." He stooped to pick up a chunk of sandstone and hurled it hard against a low-hanging branch of a mango tree just ahead. The impact turned the stone to sand. "Anyway, you people choose what you want, and I keep hoping, but in a year or two I'll be ready to give up all hope. But I'll never understand exactly what's been going wrong." Baako followed him down the gently dropping curve of the road, then along the sharp right turn to his bungalow.

When they were inside, Ocran indicated an armchair. "Sit down," he said. "I owe you an apology. The last time you came, I was in a rush."

"I know. But I didn't come for anything important. Just to say hello."

Ocran gave Baako a tall glass of beer, poured another for himself and sat on the floor with his back to the nearest wall and his legs crossed easily in front of him. "So now, Mr. Scribe, what are you going to do? Write by yourself?"

"I don't think it's possible," Baako answered. "I wouldn't want to."

"What's so impossible about doing your work alone?"

"I don't understand it fully," Baako said. "But I've thought a lot about it. In fact I went all the way round the bend trying to make up my mind."

"It doesn't hurt an artist to taste a bit of madness," Ocran said. "But I thought a decision to write would be a simple thing."

"Not for me. I had a nervous breakdown over it."

"You didn't want to write, then?" Ocran asked with a small smile.

"That's all I've been trained to do. No, that wasn't it, though I felt like I was cracking up when I first realized it fully. It was like being tricked into a trap. But the real difficulty began after I had accepted that. I couldn't decide what kind of writing I should spend my lifetime on."

"I see you have the ghost of a missionary inside you, bullying the artist." Ocran was laughing, but the statement embarrassed Baako. He put his glass to his lips, then looked through the drink and the thick glass bottom and saw a distorted image of the laughing face.

"You can look at it that way," he said finally. "Only, I was thinking of it as a way of making my life mean something to me. After all, I had to ask myself who'd be reading the things I wanted to write."

"You just depress yourself asking those questions," Ocran said.

"It happened, yes," Baako said. "But I came out of it with some sort of a decision. I wouldn't do the usual kind of writing."

"You decided to give up even that?"

"Not to give up. But if I can write for film instead of wasting my time with the other stuff — it's a much clearer way of saying things to people here."

Ocran sat staring a long time, as if he had not heard, then he said, "I know what you're saying. It looks like a hopeless picture, doesn't it? Not too many literate people. And even those who are literate won't read."

"Film gets to everyone," Baako said, and he saw the other nod gently. "In many ways, I've thought the chance of doing film scripts for an illiterate audience would be superior to writing, just as an artistic opportunity. It would be a matter of images, not words. Nothing necessarily foreign in images, not like English words."

"I understand," Ocran said. Now he was no longer nodding; he was shaking his head. "I understand, and what you say is true. But there is something I'd like to tell you. I know you'll think I'm crazy or worse. Anyway, it doesn't matter. If you want to do any work here, you have to decide quite soon that you'll work alone."

'That's impossible with film."

"I have no idea," Ocran said. "I'm antiquated, maybe. But I know definitely that you can't do anything serious here if you need other people's help, because nobody is interested in being serious."

"I don't know —" Baako said.

"No. You don't know." Ocran drained his glass and did not fill it up again. "So you're working for Ghanavision."

"Not yet," Baako answered.

"You've been back some time."

"Yes. I asked for a job more than three weeks ago. About a month now. Filled out all the necessary forms, in triplicate. I keep going to the Civil Service Commission place, and they keep telling me to go and come tomorrow."

"What!" Ocran exploded, getting up. "They're already putting you through that kind of nonsense?"

"Actually, that's what made me come here today. I went again to see someone called the Junior Assistant to the Secretary of the Civil Service Commision. He's supposed to be dealing with my papers. He told me if I wanted him to help me —"

"That's what they say when they want a bribe," Ocran muttered, running a hand over his hair and pacing the floor. "Nothing works in this country. What can you expect? The place is run by this so-called elite of pompous asses trained to do nothing. Nothing works." He turned and came back toward Baako. "When did you send in your application?"

"Three weeks ago, at least."

"It isn't even that things are slow. Nothing works. There are dozens of organizations, supposed to take care of this and that. But if you want anything done you have to go running all round these stupid organizations themselves." He walked from one end of the hall to another, first with an angry briskness and then more slowly; finally he stopped beside a desk pushed flush into a corner; it had a black telephone on it. "It all keeps coming back down to this, in the end," he said, lifting the receiver. "The organizations might just as well not exist. You keep getting pushed into using personal contacts." He turned the side handle on the old machine and said, a long pause later, "Suzie . . . Kofi Ocran here. How are you? Look, could you try and get me the Ministry of Information? It's urgent. Ask for the Principal Secretary . . . No. They'll say he's out, but say it's an urgent personal call . . . Yes . . . Thanks, Suzie." He left the telephone and returned to sit on the floor, facing Baako. He said nothing for a while, but his expression was that of a man fighting against a rising feeling of disgust and anger directed against himself.

The visit to the Principal Secretary's home was short. He was a corpulent man who laughed a lot and seemed really to enjoy doing it. He looked young, probably less than forty, and during the course of the evening he seemed unable to make up his mind whether to call Ocran *akora* or master. He had asked to see Baako at home any time after six that day, and after an early dinner Ocran had driven to his house, a large, new two-storey building in the shadow of the red triangle of lights made by the warning beacons on the grid towers at Broadcasting House. He was sitting on his front porch, slowly taking in some drink alone, when Ocran stopped in his driveway and got out with Baako. The light on the porch was green, and it lit the Principal Secretary with a weird, sickly glow as he turned up his eyes, studying Baako's face with casual interest.

"So," he said, letting out a satisfied breath of air after the greetings, "this is our returned schoolboy who doesn't know the ropes, eh?" There was a still, humid silence, which Ocran broke: "Those people at the Civil Service Commission are giving him the runaround, and there's no reason. He's a very capable man, and he's qualified."

"Yes, yes," the Principal Secretary said perfunctorily, flicking an insect off the top of his glass. His manner made it plain he thought all this was beside the point. "Sit down." He indicated a swinging sofa whose stripes of assorted colors had acquired a confusing tinge in the general green. "You're quite right, *Akora*, there's no reason. But why didn't the young man steer clear of those people anyway?"

"I assumed it was the logical thing to do," said Baako.

"Now you know better," the Principal Secretary said with a triumphant laugh. His teeth had a green filmy luster under the light.

"He seems to have done everthing there was to do." Ocran's effort to keep his anger under control was not entirely successful. "The machinery exists, and he has the training for working with it. There's something very wrong if he can be blocked like this, so stupidly."

The Principal Secretary sucked his teeth loudly and asked Ocran if he'd like something to drink. Ocran shook his head, and when Baako did the same the Principal Secretary finished sucking his teeth and said in a flat tone of voice, "We don't have modern systems here. This country doesn't work that way. If you come back thinking you can make things work in any smooth, efficient way, you'll just get a complete waste of your time. It's not worth bothering about." Ocran let out a hot sigh, but said nothing. The Principal Secretary drew his free hand across his glistening forehead and continued. "Unfortunately —" he winked at Ocran — "the young man will also be finding out that making a go of life means forgetting all the beautiful stuff they teach in the classroom. It's very different, the way things really work." Abruptly, he seemed to lose all interest in the subject; he began, instead, to ask Ocran several small questions — about his wife, his children, the new entrance requirements at the school, the next meeting of the Old Boy's Association — to all of which Ocran gave short, uninterested answers. Only at the end, about half an hour later, did the Principal Secretary return suddenly to the subject.

"Well," he said casually, "I have to go over to the River Club. Quarcoo with be there. I'll talk to him. He is the one who makes decisions at the C.S.C. In any case, you can go to Ghanavision as from tomorrow and start work. Just tell Asante-Smith you have instructions from me. You'll be paid for all the time you've lost — I'll see to that." He walked over and shook hands. "I must go and get ready for the Club. God, I feel sweaty."

Ocran drove like a drunken man, talking in his rage, careless as to where and when he cut across other lines of traffic; twice he changed gears too fast and the gearbox gave a sickening screech, but he seemed to take note of nothing. "You heard him. You're supposed to forget everything good you ever learned . . . Damn these full headlights; I can't see the side of the road . . . It's all nothing to him, and to the others like him. You'll be agreeing with him all too soon. I hate these stupid Ghanaian big shots. They know things don't work, but they're happy to sit on top of the mess all the same. Now he feels he's done us a great favor, and that's the way he wants it. You're expected to be grateful. The machinery doesn't work, except as a special favor for special cases. A chance to work . . . But they know what they're doing, in the long run. You know, Baako, what you're getting there is not a chance to do any useful work. Heaven help you if you go into that Civil Service thinking you're going to work. They sit on their bottoms doing nothing. So it's a sinecure. Things make sense. What a twisted life! But think about it. You'll have to find out what you can do alone, and go ahead and do it . . . Which way do I turn?"

A little after the Awudome cemetery Ocran swung hastily into the middle of the road and Baako heard a soft noise followed by the pained yelp of a dog. Ocran cursed and the dog howled longer and more distantly, then everything grew silent till the car stopped on the deserted street outside Baako's home.

"Thank you," he said again.

"You should come and see me more often," Ocran said.

"I'm not very mobile."

"That's true. We have a Transport Ministry, but the transportation system is a joke. Like everything else."

"Why don't you come in for a moment?"

"No, I have to go. But come to the school. It's good to see you."

"Thanks a lot."

"Good night."

"Good night."

*

Araba was very weak after her return from the hospital with the new baby, but within a day her usual appetite for peppery soups and stews and kenkey and fufu was coming back. That Wednesday Baako heard her calling him only moments after he had come back from Ghanavision; he hurried to her thinking there was something wrong, and at first it actually seemed as if the disappointed look she had had on being turned away from the shiny new ward was still there, but when Baako went to her side she smiled weakly yet with obvious happiness and made him sit on the bed beside her with both his hands in hers, and she stroked his skin gently over and over again, seeming to get an extraordinary amount of pleasure just from doing that.

"You were so good to me, Baako," she said. "I am ashamed to think of the mess I made. And in the hospital you gave me your blood."

"A pint isn't much," he said. "They give you a drink, and in an hour you're just the same."

"It wasn't the blood alone." As if she had grown suddenly shy Araba withdrew her hands and turned instead to touch the head of the baby beside her. "The child too. You gave him to me." Baako steadied himself.

"You'd better give all the credit to Kwesi. After all, he is your husband."

"You have a bad man's rotten tongue," she said, giggling and covering her mouth with her right hand. "Baako, you'll kill me if you come and make me laugh. My inside is still hollow, you know. But truly, what I meant was this: if you had not come back yourself, I would have lost this baby also.

"Is that what the baby said to you?"

"Baako, you'll destroy me. Believe the truth when you hear it. Do you know how many times I tried for this child and failed?"

"Only husbands know, no?"

"I'm going to tell you anyway. Five times." She counted fingers and thumb. "Five good times. It was when you were writing those letters which made us doubt so much whether you would come. And then you got ill."

"Yes."

"I would carry him for months, and then just as I was getting happy thinking of myself as a mother, everything would pass away in such a river of bad blood I could have died. Now see, it is such a good thing, your coming. Already you have brought me this, the baby. Other blessings will follow, that I know."

"I don't know."

"You won't ever go anywhere away from us again, Baako. Stay, and the baby will stay too. Baako, he is yours. He will be named after you."

"Isn't it the father who decides these things?"

"Ah, yes. And nothing prevents the mother from helping the

father make a good decision. Men think they rule the world," she said, smiling. "Let them think so."

"Your husband Kwesi won't agree."

"He will. You don't know as well as I do what hangs inside a man's trousers."

"You don't talk like a hollowed-out woman."

"I will bet you if you want."

"All right," Baako said.

"If you win," Araba asked, "what is your demand?"

"You'll give up the stupid outdooring ceremony or whatever it is."

"It's not stupid," she laughed. "But it's all right. I won't lose. And if I win I want only one thing: you'll be the M.C."

"The what?"

"Master of Ceremonies."

"Oh." Baako rose to go.

"Don't go," Araba said. She held him again, more tightly, and neither of them spoke. He looked past her at the baby on the bed. Babyhood, infancy, going to school . . . the thought of a person having to go through the whole cycle again brought back his nausea, and suddenly the room to him felt too humid, too full with the mother, the child and him.

His mother was beside them before he noticed her presence. When he saw her, she was staring at him and at his sister with wide, fascinated, childish eyes, and she was saying: "Ei, ei! Is it the sister wanting to make love to the brother or is it the other way round?"

"The male falls in the female trap; the woman is always cleverer," said Araba, at the same time relaxing her hold. The presence of another person with her seemed to have reassured her and driven away the plain fear she had of being left alone with the child; her body lost its tension, and she was able to sink back completely into the softness of the bed and pillows underneath her. It was the mother's face that had tension in it now.

"It's so tiring, having to deal with the children," she said.

"You won't have to continue long," said Araba, "now that Baako has come. It's the time you've waited for." Baako felt a strong kind of pressure in the back of his head, together with an unpleasant awareness that in some way he was expected to fill the long silence that followed with words, with promises, perhaps. He could say nothing, and his discomfort was deepening into something scarcely bearable. Then he heard his mother speaking to his sister.

"Araba, perhaps you are still too weak to think of this, but have you considered that this impatient child chose a very bad time to arrive?"

"His coming has made me so happy I wouldn't have it any other way now," said Araba.

Baako saw the look on his mother's face take on a sudden severity.

"That's not what I'm talking about." She paused, then said with irritation, "I mean the outdooring." Araba looked completely surprised and uncomprehending, but the moment passed and she looked as if something important had reached her understanding, and she also sat silent and pensive, looking at her mother.

"You see?" asked the mother.

"Yes, yes," Araba nodded.

"So this is what I think should be done . . ."

"What is this mysterious thing you're talking about?" Baako asked. "Or shouldn't I know?"

"It's nothing mysterious," his mother said, offhand.

"You men are not supposed to be concerned with these things of the earth," Araba said archly. "Has Naana never told you what a man is? Listen." She laughed. "Man is pure spirit and should be free and untouched, and it is only for a little while that he comes down to live in a body borrowed from us women, the females of the race, living trapped like sunlight that goes into a house through a window or into the earth through a hole." She was laughing so much her happiness was beginning to turn into pain, and she stopped herself. "So men should be spirits, ghosts, according to Naana."

For some reason the turn the conversation had taken seemed to have displeased Efua, and she was quiet for a while.

"This is the third day since our little stranger chose to come," she said finally. "Baako, can we have the calendar?" Baako went to the left side wall and took down the huge calendar from off its hook. The calendar itself was a small thing suspended from a very large color picture advertising something called AMBI-EXTRA skin-lightening cream. In the center foreground stood a couple of Africans with successfully bleached skins looking a forced yellow-brown. Around them several darker Africans stood in various poses, all open-mouthed with admiration of the bleached pair.

Efua took the calendar, got momentarily lost in admiring contemplation of the picture, then turned her gaze down to the calendar itself.

"I've already forgotten today's date," she said.

"September twenty-eighth," Baako said.

"The month is almost dead," Efua said. "Wednesday . . . This is such a bad time. But we'll have to think seriously about the outdooring ceremony."

"I thought there were fixed times for those things," Baako said. "Like a week or a month or whatever it is after birth?" Neither his mother or his sister seemed to have been listening.

"An outdooring ceremony held more than a few days after payday is useless," Efua said.

"Totally," Araba agreed with great enthusiasm. "Ghanaian men get broke so fast these days it isn't funny."

"You're right," said Efua. "The only sensible time is the first weekend after payday."

"So when is payday this month?" Araba asked.

"I'm not very sure," said Efua.

"For Senior Officers, September 26," Baako intoned, making no attempt to purge the sarcasm from his voice, "for Junior Officers, September 29; for laborers, October 3. I read it on our official board at work." The sarcasm was let drip harmlessly away.

"The eighth day after his homecoming would be . . . the fourth," Araba said.

"No," Baako answered, affecting an infant's voice. "Thirty days hath September . . ."

"So would it be the fifth?"

"Yes."

"Fourth, Tuesday, fifth, Wednesday," Efua said dejectedly. "Both are useless days. Sunday is the second."

"Sunday, then," said Araba.

"Why are you struggling so with the calendar?" Baako asked. "Are you so pressed you have to make money out of the child?"

"Ei, son," his mother said sharply, "we don't need you to preach at us."

Baako closed his mouth and sat staring at the baby, listening to the two women talking, remaining outside their plans.

"Can we manage?" Araba asked.

"Don't worry. I'll arrange everything," her mother answered.

"But are you sure Kwesi will agree?"

"I'll make him agree."

"How?"

"I have my secret weapon."

"Where?"

Araba pointed in the direction of her genitals and said languidly, "Here."

"Ah, you're so rotten."

"It's you who wanted to see my secret weapon." They laughed.

"You talk. The way the baby left you all torn up inside, you won't be in any position to use that weapon for a long while."

"That's why it's going to be effective. You know, the midwife says Kwesi should leave me alone for two months. If he doesn't agree to the things I'm going to ask for, I'll add another month. Think of his big *kojo* going hungry for three long months."

"Araba," the mother laughed, "you're going to drive some woman's son crazy."

"Let him starve a bit. After all, we have to find some way of making men share some of all this suffering. They can't always come in and pump it in and goodbye and leave us with all the work."

"Be careful, Araba," Efua said. "Men turn vultures and look for what they need in the street if they can't find it at home."

"Not my Kwesi," said Araba. "He's told me the only sweet food he knows grows between my thighs. I'm not afraid."

"You are lucky," Efua said. "If I were you —" But at that moment the ouside gate was heard swinging open, and she got up. "It's your husband, Araba. I have to go. He'll think there's a family plot against him."

"Oh, no," Araba said after her mother, "he knows Baako is always on his side."

Kwesi came in carrying a bulky package and grinning self-consciously. He looked for a space near Araba and deposited the package there.

"What is that?" Araba said.

"Patience," Kwesi said, peeling off the white packaging, his back turned to his wife. When he was through he wheeled round suddenly and showed her the gift: an electric fan with strong, long blades and a chromium casing on a base of metallic gray, with three different buttons for working it and a long connecting cord.

"Oh, the fan," Araba said with explosive joy, then checked herself and placed her right hand on her abdomen. "Oh, Kwesi, thank you very much. So many lucky things happening to me all at once." She was smiling, but out of a corner of her eye Baako could see a tear slide down. Then, almost immediately, he saw his sister wink and look toward the door, and he knew she wanted him out so she could go to work on her husband. He walked out quietly and went into his room.

Images of men with guns hunting frightened birds flying above savanna trees and the killing embrace of enemy insects crushing each other's exoskeletons and squeezing out the pulp of life within in the unending destructiveness of life were filing across his mind when he heard someone knock.

"Come." He did not stop reading till he came to the end of a paragraph.

"Oh, you're reading," he heard Kwesi say. "Sorry." But he had come to the end of the paragraph. He inserted a pencil to mark the page and closed the book.

"No, stay," he said, sitting up on the bed and indicating the chair in front of him: "Sit down. I don't have to finish it all at once."

"It's a big book," Kwesi said. The desembodied eyes on the cover stared directly as Baako looked at them, radiating in their intensity some other kind of message to supplement the title and the author's name:

DORIS LESSING: THE GOLDEN NOTEBOOK.

"What news?" asked Baako, trying to smile. His brother-in-law looked sad.

"Can you come with me?" he pleaded. "I need a drink. Outside."

They went down the hill to the Winneba junction and then crossed from the Orbit Cinema side to the right and turned left and walked till they came to the CAFE OF THE SILVER SHOOTING STAR. It was new but already the owner was known to everyone inside as a good friend and several of them shoved him gently in the belly and called him Big Bontoss on account of his fatness. Kwesi chose a table near the farthest side where there was not too much light and the tables were not so close together, and when the barman came he ordered a Star beer for himself and Baako asked for a bottle of ginger ale and saw the barman smile in unresentful condescension down at him. Before the drinks arrived Kwesi was already shaking his head and saying softly, "I find it so difficult to go against the wishes of a woman once I'm facing her. I'm never sure if they are wrong, or if what they say is true. In the end I agree all the same." The barman brought the drinks and turned to go. Through the entrance came a young man with a beautiful face that looked sad in spite of its freshness, and he was wearing very tight trousers and a black shirt with a thin white line running across the top of his pocket. In the bright entrance light his eyes looked red and his face a very smooth black.

"Ei, Bukari," the barman shouted, "is that you?"

"Yes, Bontoss, it's me again." The young man's tone was very dejected.

"What will you have?" It seemed as if the barman was deliberately raising the level of mirth in his own voice to cheer the young man up.

"Give me whatever you want, but make sure it kills me quick." The table the young man selected was only a yard or two from Baako's.

"You will have to choose your own death, Bukari," the barman said with a loud laugh that spread to the crowd within and produced a‾ proving cries of "True, too true!" "Gin, Whisky? Rum? Schnapps?"

"Anything . . . whisky!" the young man made up his mind. In a moment the barman was beside him with a bottle of whisky and a glass. When he shouted to a waitress called Grace to bring some ice and water, the young man waved him away, saying, "No. No water today." With a crazy swiftness the young man filled his glass and drank the whisky straight, then went through the whole process twice over. The barman grabbed his hands.

"What has happened, Bukari?" he asked. "What is the trouble?" There was no answer. "It is not good to drink so swiftly and silently, suffering alone like that." Still there was no answer. The barman took the bottle with the remainder of the whisky in it and started for his counter. There was now a silence in the place and all the other drinkers had lost their smiles, their eyes turned on the young man and the barman with him. The young man sprang up and in a sudden, unexpected explosion of violent energy he turned the barman round with an irresistible rough power and snatched the bottle from him.

"Leave the bottle," he said, "I have nothing else." He began to pour himself another glass of the pure drink, and at that moment Baako heard his brother-in-law.

"You know what Araba said to me."

"Yes. What was your decision?"

"Things are so difficult . . . so confusing," Kwesi said. "You know what she wants."

"She said she was going to ask you."

"It was so difficult. When she said everybody does it, I didn't know what more to say."

"This baby was premature. You have to take special care," Baako said.

"True," Kwesi said, "and yet . . . and yet . . ."

The noise of splintering glass made Baako turn. The young man Bukari had given his table a push, and the glass and the bottle on it had shattered on the floor, spilling the dregs. Almost simultaneously, before any of the other watching drinkers could rise to go to his help, the young man slumped off his chair. His head hit the edge of his table and then bounced off it onto the floor. He was in no position to break his fall. He dropped with inert heaviness, his face hitting the floor right on top of the shards from the broken glass and the whisky bottle. A woman, a little drunk herself, reached him first and tried to raise him. She was only able to raise his head a foot or so above the floor, and then it fell back down and the woman began to weep loudly at the sight of all that blood beginning to flow from the young man's face. Now three men reached him and raised him up, and he groaned as they tried to pick out the larger pieces of glass imbedded in his face.

"Oh my mother!" the young man said, unable to stand by himself.

"Oh, Great Friend," the weeping woman said, "the poor child. There has been a death in his family." The young man was taken to a safer table and when they sat him down his head came to rest on top of the table and he stayed like that sobbing a long time. Then something seemed to have revived him a bit and he put his right hand in his trouser pocket but found nothing there and then he reached up into the shirt pocket with the thin white line edging the black and from it he drew a pinkish brown envelope and stared at it a long time without even opening it. After that he began to shout and weep. "I have traveled and suffered and it was all for you. Doing work and taking insults into my throat and running near my hope. Next year at Christmas I would have come back and given you many things you have dreamed about but never had. Did I not tell you? Was I a bad son to you? Why did you have to go so hatefully just when I was getting ready to come again? What have I done that you should have thought to do this thing to me? What did I do to you that was wrong?"

The woman went over and put her hand on the young man's head, but her companion came and pulled her away, saying, "You leave him alone. Let him go deep in his sorrow. That is the only way."

"Another drink!" the young man shouted suddenly, his head still on the table, his hand raised in a crooked call. The barman took a plastic glass and mixed some more whisky with water before takng it to the young man's table.

"The drink will kill him." the weeping woman said.

"It will not," said the barman, putting the plastic glass beside the head on the bloody table. "Bukari needs a little of the ghost of death now. He must forget. He won't have money to pay for this, but he's my friend, Bukari." The young man groped upward with his left hand till it grasped the glass, trembling lightly.

"The trouble is," Kwesi was saying, keeping his eyes averted from the sufferer at the bloody table, "once we begin talking, nothing is clear any more. She tells me we have to do this thing and that thing because everybody does them, and I can't say it's a lie."

"I still bet Araba you wouldn't agree to her demands," Baako said.

"Yes." Kwesi drank his beer and refilled his glass. "She told me afterwards."

"Well . . ." Baako smiled into his glass. "I lost." He drank the few remaining drops of his ginger ale.

"Shall we go? I've paid the barman," Kwesi said. Baako nodded. They went carefully past the young man, who seemed to be sleeping. The last scratchy verse of an old song was coming out of the loudspeaker near the door.

> If you didn't looove me dear,
> Why didn't you leeet me knooow?

When it ended an old high life replaced it almost immediately. It had a very fast, very joyful beat, with guitar sounds that could have been meant for laughter or for tears, and then the words began:

> Tomorrow I'll be gone,
> Bluebottle flies swarming over me . . .

The weeping woman had stopped her weeping and was standing in front of her companion, asking him to come and dance the high life with her.

"Sit down," her companion said with irritation. "You women are so crazy."

The woman curled her upper lip in contempt. "And every man thinks it was he who made the world. Look, this music is nice, isn't it? And as for death, when we came down it was here already, so let me live if you won't." She moved to the center, oblivious of all around, and started dancing all by herself to the music.

> I'll be away tomorrow
> giving life to worms.
> Tomorrow I'll be dead,
> vultures flying over my roof,
> where I am only a stranger
> so stranger,
> let me play my game.
> Stranger,
> let me dance my dance.

"It's this Sunday, the child's outdooring," Kwesi said after they had passed the Winneba crossroads.

"I know," Baako answered.

This Sunday morning the sound that awakened him was the repeated early bleating of the ram tethered to the last mango tree in the yard outside. It had been brought specially from the village Kotse-ye-Aboa — the ancestral home he had been to just once, very long ago, by a man whom everybody called Korankye the Hunchback — to be killed and eaten in the celebration of the new child's entry into this world above. Then for some time the sound from the animal was mixed with noises from people going to the lavatory and the bathroom and getting ready for the day's ceremony. He lay in bed till after he had heard his mother singing to herself as she took out the tablecloths and the borrowed glasses and new cutlery and left them on the porch near his room; when she had finished he went out in shorts and a singlet past the porch with the three tables and the pink and blue tablecloths on them under the rows of bottles of drinks already in place before the armchairs arranged in front for the VIP guests and the Cinema hall chairs, red, green and gold, set out in the yard for the others. In the back, away from the tree to which the ram had been tied, five coal pots stood ready with the coal beginning to glow a dark red, giving off barely perceptible little flames of blue and yellow in the centers of the heaps in the pots.

From inside the kitchen where he had spent the night Korankye the Hunchback advanced blinking against the soft light of the morning. In his left hand he held a green beer bottle with an open top from which the smell of *akpeteshie* gin rose and remained in the air like a hanging mist; his right hand clutched two things — a long steel knife with a wooden handle, and an iron file to sharpen it. He was taking short but frequent swigs from the bottle, throwing back his head and emitting a strong grunt after each mouthful swallowed, as if the liquid had burned some of the lining inside his throat and chest.

"Morning, master," he said when he saw Baako.

"Korankye, I am not your master," Baako said. Korankye the Hunchback laughed at him and tipped his head back for another swallow before he reached the tree with the tethered ram. There he stood regarding the animal, his head rising and falling in its drunken nodding, while from time to time a short cry would escape from his throat, a sound that was a weird combination of amazed fear and a chuckle of contempt. The hunchback touched the animal roughly and put his drink down on the ground, on the other side of the tree; then he took the file in his free left hand and for a time sharpened the long knife against its roughness. At last he was satisfied with the knife's sharpness, having run his thumb along it in a movement that had in it nothing of a drunkard's carelessness. He raised the knife upward, aiming the point of it at the sky, and said: "Nananom, this is me, Korankye, and I am about to spill blood." In one smooth, semicircular motion he brought the knife down and plunged it firmly a few inches into the brown sand and earth. He reached for his bottle and poured some drops down from where he stood, spattering the knife.

"Drink, Nananom, and understand your child," he said. He emptied what was left in the bottle into his own throat, choked and belched powerfully with it, and beat himself upon the chest several times before he could bring his coughing to a stop; throwing the bottle over the yard wall, he bent down and pulled the knife out of the ground and moved toward the animal. It tried to run, but the hunchback pulled strongly on its rope and brought it down in front of himself, answering its bleating with his own hard-breathing silence. When he had firmly trapped the animal, pressing upon its forelegs with his full weight balanced on his right foot, he looked again at the sky, spat in his right palm and rubbed it in the sand, then took a final grip on the knife. The ram shook as the hunchback stroked its throat with the knife, wiping off the dust, and it had time for one long hoarse cry when he grasped its head and pushed it as far back as it would go before slashing quickly at its throat and opening it. First the blood sprang out, but in a while the pressure behind it eased and it flowed out more easily, taking a gentle, pulsing, dying rhythm. Korankye the hunchback reached up and tore off the leaves from the lowest hanging branch of the mango tree and with them wiped the ram's blood off his knife. After that he raised the dead animal and staggered with it toward the fires; in a moment the back of the yard was filled with the rising smoke and the smell of burning hair and flesh, and the hunchback added the sharp screech of metal on metal as he sharpened other knives for the cutting he would have to do.

Baako went in through the door that led from the back veranda. The bathroom was free so he took a quick shower after shaving and he had gone back to his room and almost finished dressing when a soft knock sounded on his door and he answered it. It was his grandmother who came in, saying what she had come to say even before she was fully inside the room.

"There have been such strong smells this morning."

"Sit down, Naana," Baako said. "The chair is just to your left."

"I know," the old woman said, sitting down. "Such terrible smells," she said again; then a smile crossed her frown. "But I must say I like the smell here. Powder and lavender."

"I just shaved," said Baako.

"But those other smells. Sounds, too. I heard an animal die this morning in the yard."

"It was a ram."

"Which ram?"

"Araba's son is coming out today," Baako answered.

"But that is not possible," she said. "Or have I lost count of my days all over again? Is it then a week since your sister came back with the child?"

"You have not lost count, Naana. It's five days now, but it's been decided. This is to be the day."

"Five days," the old woman whispered in her astonishment. "Five days. The child is not yet with us. He is in the keeping of the spirits still, and already they are dragging him out into this world for eyes in heads that have eaten flesh to gape at."

"Araba wanted it that way," Baako said. "My mother too, and in the end Kwesi also agreed to it."

"The child is one of the uncertain ones. If he stays he may bring great things." His grandmother shook her head. "They themselves say he refused the world several times. And it should have made them think, the way he finally came. He was weeks before his time."

"Yes, Naana."

"Baako, how can I say what is in my soul? Often a quick child like that is only a disturbed spirit come to take a brief look and go back home. But I am too old. Let me say this to them and inside their hearts they will accuse me, calling me a witch who would take the infant life just to lengthen mine."

"No one will think such thoughts of you," said Baako.

"You are still young, and you know little of the forest people have for their souls. But that is good; you have enough youth in you to make you generous." Naana sighed, then leaned forward. "And you, what do you say to all this masquerade?"

"Nothing," Baako answered. "I do not fully understand the ceremony itself."

"Ah, that is a shame. The ceremony you ought to understand, or where do you get the meaning of it, even if it is done right? Don't you see? You know the child is only a traveler between the world of spirits and this one of heavy flesh. His birth can be a good beginning, and he may find his body and this world around it a home where he wants to stay. But for this he must be protected. Or he will run screaming back, fleeing the horrors prepared for him up here. How is it that you do not understand that?"

"I should listen more to you, Naana," Baako said, making his smile audible, "but always I find you so sad."

"Don't try to soften me with sweet words, Baako," his grandmother said. "Why did you not stop your sister and your mother also from this foolishness?"

"I could not."

"Now it is my turn not to understand. You, the uncle, you could not?"

"I thought Kwesi would stop Araba," Baako said, "but I was wrong. And he is the father."

"Was there any need to tell me that? Kwesi is the father. I have heard you. But the child is yours to look after. A father is only a husband, and husbands come and go; they are passing winds bearing seed. They change, they disappear entirely, and they are replaced. An uncle remains. The blood that flows in Araba is yours, Baako, and the child is yours also if it is hers. So what has he done, that you will fold your arms and let them destroy him?"

"Naana," Baako said with some irritation, "I understand what you have said, but the world has changed. I am only a relative. I cannot stop them from doing what they want with their own child."

"The world has changed . . ." the old woman murmured, then raised her voice. "Always and everywhere the same words that bring a sickness to the stomach of the listener. The world has changed . . . And they think it is enough to explain every new crime, to push a person to accept all. Listen, Baako, I should tell you this —"

She stopped so suddenly it was only after his mother had knocked and entered that Baako realized his grandmother had felt the approaching steps. And when his mother saw his grandmother in the room she frowned and asked with obvious anger, "What is troubling you, Naana?" For a moment the old woman sat like a person held there by some huge terror and made inarticulate by a deep loathing. Then she rose, and after answering slowly, "Nothing, Efua, I am not troubled," she went out without having to stretch out her hands to find the door.

"What was she here for?" his mother asked.

"Just to talk," Baako answered. A suspicious look came on his mother's face, lingered a while and went away.

"Anyway," she said, "you know you're the M.C. today."

"Yes. What do I have to do?"

"I am not the one who has been abroad to a university," his mother said, smiling full into his face.

"What I went to learn was different," he said.

"Well, there won't be too much to do. I wish you had brought a tux, or at least a suit, though. It would have been so fine."

"I'm not an ape."

"What a strange thing to say!" his mother said.

"Why else would I wear tuxes and suits in this warm country except to play monkey to the white man?"

"But for a special ceremony like this . . ."

"I suppose your sacred ancestors laid down the word that we should sweat in stupid suits and tuxes for such ceremonies. Too bad. I'm going to wear clothes that won't choke me."

"Oh, Baako," his mother said, with real hurt in her voice, "I was only thinking of the best. Baako, what happened to you?"

"What do you mean?" he asked. But his mother was looking at him as if what she was staring at was something behind him, something that she could see only by looking through him.

"Nothing," she said. "You will receive the guests and later you can give them drinkables. Serve the VIP's first."

"Is that all?"

"Yes," his mother answered, turning to go. "Oh, and also, take care of the collection." Before he could say anything, she had left, closing the door very softly after her.

5 : Osagyefo

SHE HAD EXPECTED the throbbing in her temple to cease in a matter of moments, but long after the man had left her office Juana continued to feel this uncomfortable pulse getting stronger. It spread its quality over the whole of her head, then into her body, and at times it was hard to separate it from the flickering on-off-on tempo of the two long tubes of fluorescent light above her desk. Indeterminate at first, the hum gradually approached understandable sound: a soft and steady vibration saying you you you you you you.

She knew she was tired, but even as she stared at the blurred notes in front of her, wanting to stop trying to understand what had happened this afternoon, she caught herself beginning again the futile attempts at self-persuasion, at certainty, as though she needed to believe there was no reason why she should have reacted any other way. And yet the man himself had not seemed visibly concerned about what he was in relation to her. A patient come to see a doctor, a man face to face with a woman, a stranger talking across a desk to another stranger, or perhaps to a possible friend: everything about his attitude was unfixed, free-floating, potential. And all of it disturbed her.

It was unpleasant, the suspicion that in spite of everything she thought she believed, she was herself not free in any way from the comforting pigeonholing reflex, and that she had surprised herself now in the process of reaching back for refuge in that habit, searching for the ease of dealing with a patient, pushing back the threat of having to confront another human being.

She had tried not to think of the choice, but it came up anyway and occupied her mind. She could treat him safely and simply as a patient — go on living shut up in her own loneliness, leave him in his, know she had been defending herself behind a sentimental piece of fiction she had woven for herself, nothing worse, nothing better, this idea that she had been hungering to treat people as human beings and to have them treat her the same way. She could do this, refuse to be anything outside her professional self; she would also have to push down her own urge to go out to him, her already growing, pulsing half-answer to his understated demand for her friendship. It could be done, and probably much more easily than thinking about it would make it seem. Or she could decide after all to follow her idea itself in its dangerous freedom, take the stranger's invitation all the way into friendship, risk closeness in a situation and a place that could so easily turn his lucidity into some vertiginous disease, unless he took great care, or like the young doctor she had once known, found survival by shedding this painful ability to see so clearly.

Yet in truth she was not so sure whether the decision was still hers to make. The young man, when he walked in, had a relaxed, detached air that was almost offensively nonchalant. He shook hands without any kind of noticeable expression and waited till she told him to sit. He sat there not looking at her, saying nothing until she asked him why he had come to her; then he answered it was to see about a routine checkup. She had an impulse to laugh. She took the papers he was holding out to her, noted his name and age and the fact that he worked for Ghanavision, and smiled at him.

"Have they gotten so modern they ask all their new men to come for a checkup?" she asked.

"No," he replied without smiling. "I wasn't asked to come. I came on my own." She was about to ask him why, but she saw him pointing at the second sheet he had given her, and she took it up and studied it carefully. It was a report written by a doctor to be contacted, if necessary, at an address in New York. She scribbled down the medication indicated in his treatment, hesitated, then wrote down the address also just in case it ever became necessary. She looked at the man again, and absently mentioned his name. He did not answer, but now his eyes were meeting hers, a patient, almost bored look in them.

"So you were put on Thorazine," she said.

"Yes."

"What was it you had? LSD trouble?"

He shook his head. "I had a friends who were taking it, but I didn't get round to trying it myself. Why?"

"This drug you were given," she said, "it's been used to counteract the consciousness expansion effect."

"I see. I didn't know," he said. "But I remember once he told me, the doctor, that I must be generating my own expansion toxins."

"It's possible, but it's not very common. So you're one of the . . ." she tried to check herself and failed ". . . lucky few?"

"I wouldn't call it lucky." His tone was flat, so hostile that it lacked even the warmth of anger, and Juana thought briefly of an apology, before she looked again at him and saw it would be a waste of time.

"It should take an awful lot of anxiety to produce the effect spontaneously," she said after a while. "What was on your mind?"

"Many things."

"I suppose so," she said, "but mainly?"

"The worst thing was the fear of the return," he said.

"What was frightening about it?"

"I didn't know if I'd be able to do anything worthwhile."

"Has your uncertainty decreased since you came back?"

"I don't know. I don't think so. No." He was not the flat, hostile stranger anymore; he was looking directly at her, and she thought she could see in his eyes an intense desire to have her hear what he was beginning to tell her.

"Things are getting more definite now," he began. He talked, very precisely, of the things worrying him, like a doctor probing into a diseased body, locating a node of sickened nerves; all his talk was of a loneliness from which he was finding it impossible to break, of the society he had come back to and the many ways in which it made him feel his aloneness. She asked him about his family, thinking of some possible shelter, but when he spoke of it, his family became only a closer, intenser, more intimate reflection of the society itself, a concave mirror, as he called it, and before long she was left in no doubt at all that in many ways he saw more small possibilities of hope in the larger society than in the family around him.

"And yet," he was saying, "the family is always there, with a solid presence and real demands."

"Demands that go against those of the larger society?" she asked.

"Well, yes, in a very complicated way," he said, but instead of going on he made a gesture as if to say that anything else he might say would be useless.

"You don't find working for the family a reasonable hope?" She was trying to trap the idea, to prevent it from escaping.

"It's necessary," he said. "I can understand that. But it's changed into something else, something very deeply set now, I think. The member of the family who goes out and comes back home is a sort of charmed man, a miracle worker. He goes, he comes back, and with his return some astounding and sudden change is expected."

"Is this a new thing, do you think?" she asked him, "or something with old roots?"

"Now it's taken this modern form. The voyage abroad, everything that follows; it's very much a colonial thing. But the hero idea itself is something very old. It's the myth of the extraordinary man who brings about a complete turnabout in terrible circumstances. We have the old heroes who turned defeat into victory for the whole community. But these days the community has disappeared from the story. Instead, there is the family, and the hero comes and turns its poverty into sudden wealth. And the external enemy isn't the one at whose expense the hero gets his victory; he's supposed to get rich, mainly at the expense of the community."

"You regret the fact that you studied abroad, then?"

"No," he said, laughing. "The same things worry those who stayed here and went to Legon or Kumasi or Cape Coast. Not so fiercely, perhaps, but I've seen some of these fellows. They talk some, and do a lot of drinking. Purposeless, like to keep away things they daren't face. Spend money like some kind of suicide."

"Does all this leave you confused?"

"It's not confusion. I know what I'm expected to be." He paused, and she kept herself from interrupting. "It's not what I want to be."

She was expecting him to go on, to add something, but he did not, and she noted her own embarrassment at the small silence.

"Well, it's a good thing," she said, "you know where you're going. Your mind is made up."

"I don't know," he said.

"You're going against a general current," she said, and he nodded, his face showing practically no emotion. "It takes a lot of strength."

Now he laughed, a laugh like a cough, as though he had tried hard not to laugh, but the reaction had forced itself out against all his effort. His face was trapped in a smile so sick-looking that she was embarrassed into looking away. "If it were a current," he said. Again he left the thought incomplete.

"You don't think it is?" she asked.

"Yes, I see it," he said, relaxing. "Yes. As a matter of fact it's beginning to look like a cataract to me."

The word struck her as strange, and she wrote it down, the final *t* stretching itself out on her pad into a long horizontal line that turned back near the end of the sheet and ended in a tight clean spiral with a dot for its center. "A curious word," she let the thought out. "Why cataract?"

"It's the word that came. Why not?" he asked her back.

"No reason." She put her pencil down and it rolled slightly before its clip stopped it on the table. "I would have thought more readily of a waterfall."

Now he was laughing easily, with obvious enjoyment. "Oh no!" he said, with an exaggerated shake of his head, "I'm not a very dramatic person."

She let the statement go though she had not got out all the things the word cataract had made her want to say. She was thinking of him, and thinking of him she forgot his physical presence out there in front of her, and he became for her instead a kind of interior dome floating slowly somewhere in her head, and she had the impression she could see a small but very vital blind spot which broke into the wholeness of the dome, yet without which it would quite simply fall apart. But suddenly he was reminding her that he was there, real and physical too. He had extended his left hand a little way across the table toward her, holding between thumb and fingers a card with an elongated ceremonial mask drawn along one side of it, the remaining space taken up by black print that gradually arranged itself into words and an invitation.

"It says writers," she said uncertainly.

"And artists and one or two friends," she heard him read out in a high, mocking voice. "Will you be my friend?" He had dropped to an ordinary tone.

The suddenness of the invitation made her raise her eyes to look at him. It was not a joke he had made. He was staring at her, calmly, steadily. It was a direct look in which she could find neither entreaty alone nor challenge: the look of a man saying he was prepared for acceptance just as he was ready to be disappointed, as though the difference, to him, would not in the long run matter unduly. There was a desperation here that was so deep it was beginning to be indistinguishable from hope.

Her own eyes must have expressed amazement first, and then perhaps pleasure, acceptance; because he smiled at her, said again that it would not be till the next weekend, Saturday, and promised to meet her outside the Drama Studio and take her in. Already his mood had changed. The thought of the meeting seemed to have brought him some happiness.

"You're expecting to find something there." She had meant it as a question, and now she wondered if he would answer.

"I want to wait and see," he said.

"I've been to something like that here, once," she began. "The invitation looked very similar, identical, almost, except that where you have the mask there was a linguist's staff that time." But then she thought there was no call to talk to him like this now, so she stopped, and moments later he was shaking her hand, holding it longer than he needed to to say goodbye and leave her.

*

There was practically no one else around when she arrived. She did not drive to the wide park in front of the Studio, but stopped underneath the dark mass made by the overhanging branches and foliage of a tall nim tree by the side of the building. She remained seated in her car watching the advancing and crossing lights of cars and buses and lorries passing along the airport road under the soft green light of the AMBASSADOR sign high up on the hotel roof across the road. When there were gaps in the traffic she could see the curved stream of thin fountain water playing around the base of the entrance sign, lit up by its spotlight in a way that made it look at that distance like a molded piece of solid, clear glass. Then the cars of the others coming began to arrive, raising a mist of dust that hid the distant fountain as they slowed down and parked. From the cars people she had seen before descended and walked across to the Studio entrance. The sight of these familiar forms pulled her reluctantly into the defeating feeling of permanence, of change-lessness, the feeling she found herself still hoping to evade. A sports car sputtered by and went to a noisy stop somewhere on the opposite side of the Studio. Its driver came back minutes later, holding out a long, thin arm, jerky with a manic energy, and poking it at Juana through the car window.

"Ei Doctor!" the young man shouted at her. "Long time no see. Welcome, welcome. Where did you go?"

"I've been busy," she answered.

"Always busy," he said. He was still holding on to her hand, swinging it occasionally with an obvious, playful violence. "Always always."

"Look Lawrence," she said finally, chuckling, "let go of my hand. You'll tear my arm off."

"Sorry," the young man said. Then he laughed. "You're a tough woman, Doctor, I can't tear your arm off. You're a tough Doctor, everybody knows."

"So you think," she said, turning her head and looking again straight ahead at the hotel lights across the road.

"Trekking to the regions again?" the young man asked.

"Yes."

"Where did you go?"

"All over, Lawrence," she said. "All over the country."

"Brong Ahafo region?"

"I passed through there," she said. "I had to go north." She wished the young man wouldn't want to talk so much, but suddenly he had bent down to bring his head level with hers and was talking to her, his voice still loud but wound up now with something like the tight quality of a whisper.

"Don't let them waste your time, Doctor. Don't kill yourself trying to work against the stupid people in your Ministry. No matter what you do, they'll spoil it."

"You've been drinking," she said, with a laugh.

"So that's what you are also saying, Doctor eh? And I thought you were my friend. All right, you too have disappointed me."

"Well, Lawrence, am I wrong?"

"Wrong or right, it doesn't matter!" he shouted. Then in a calm tone he added, "You are the one who's wrong. You think I told you what I said because I had gin in my blood. Doctor, I like you but you're wrong yourself." He stood there staring at her through the open car window. The whites of his eyes showed large and softly visible in the darkness. "And anyway," he broke out again after a while, "do you know one, just one honest man who doesn't drink? You drink too, no?"

"Of course, Lawrence. What are you so upset about?"

"You know. Lawrence Boateng is a drunkard, Lawrence Boateng drinks too much. I'm tired of people talking about me. I drink, yes. I see the truth when I'm drunk, and I can say what I see. Is that wrong, Doctor?"

"You call me Doctor even when you can see the truth," she said. "My name is Juana."

"How can I call you Juana when you call me a drunkard?" He laughed and shook the car so that it rocked slightly. To the left a car door thudded shut and simultaneously its yellow taxi lights went on as it turned back down the road. The man who had come down from the taxi walked hurriedly, making for the Studio entrance; when he reached the car, Juana got out and called him. "Baako?" He came back, shook hands and apologized.

"You're not late," Juana said. "Only a few people have arrived. Do you know each other?"

"I'm Lawrence Boateng."

"Onipa. Baako Onipa."

"Mr. Onipa works for Ghanavision," Juana said.

"I've heard of you, Mr. Boateng," Baako said, shaking hands.

"I know. Everybody thinks I'm the editor of *Jungle* magazine. Secretly speaking, though, I'm only a kind of subeditor. The fools in London do what they like with my stuff before they print it. Ah, this life."

"We should be going in now," Juana said.

"The place is empty," Boateng answered. "Does Mr. Onipa know the others?"

"Which others?" Baako asked.

"I see," said Boateng. "You don't know. Look, Juana, why don't we stay here a while and watch people arrive? I can give this stranger my portraits of our local literary and artistic big shots."

"Oh no, Lawrence, he doesn't need your poison."

"I swear I'll stick to the truth."

"Editors know how to do strange things with the truth."

"Doctor, don't do that," Boateng said, adopting a hurt tone. "You're turning this stranger against me. He could be a friend, you know." Then a sudden excitement seemed to seize him, making him lose interest in what he had been saying. "Hey, look there!"

Along the drive a car advanced behind dimmed headlights, turned and crossed the dust-soft park in front, and when it stopped let out two figures that were at first hard to distinguish.

"The Cultural Empire Loyalists are early tonight," Boateng said.

"The who?" Baako asked.

"Stop being facetious and tell him who people are, Lawrence. He doesn't know, and you're playing your stale jokes." But Boateng did not seem in any way disturbed.

"Look well, stranger," he said to Baako. "The one like a pregnant slug, the one behind; that is the husband. The upright worm is his wife."

"When will you stop making nasty cracks at them?" Juana asked, but Boateng ignored her question.

"They're the British Council's married team here. Janet and James Scalder. She married him seven years ago because she thought she'd found the greatest Shakespearean actor of modern times in him."

"Oh shut up, Lawrence," Juana said, laughing against her own will. "How did you get to know why she married him?"

"It's a good story; don't spoil it," Boateng said, laughing a short, high laugh that ended like a shriek in the night. "Now he lives here for the British Council. Every year for four days he stars in a revival of *Julius Caesar* stage-managed by his wife. He plays Caesar. Oh Christ!" The last expression came out aburptly, unexpectedly, leaving a silence in its wake, as though something he hadn't dared to think about too closely had briefly appeared to the speaker.

Three cars passed and he did not break his silence. Juana thought of the young man Boateng and the way he always talked: wildly, as though he had made a conscious decision to keep touching with his words the deep bottom of things no one else wanted to think about. Was this erratic sharpness just something wild and random, or a deliberately disordered keenness? She was becoming ill at ease in the silence.

"Let's go in," she said. Boateng broke out of his silence as suddenly as he had let it engulf him.

"Wait," he said, "I haven't finished, and there's no hurry. There's Asante-Smith. But you know him already. Strange, only two girls with him this night. He's being careful."

A large University bus came and about a dozen men and women descended from it, talking and laughing. One of them kept singing just one short phrase over and over again in a deep soft bass that brought images of black velvet cloth to her mind and left them there. Then all at once a stream of cars came in, creating so much confusion and noise in the park that Boateng forgot about his verbal portraits and Juana moved wordlessly with Baako and him into the Studio.

Inside, chairs were arranged in six loose rows facing the small stage; on the stage itself there was a table with three chairs arranged in a little obtuse triangle behind it, and the intensity of two arc lights bathed the stage in a steady glare and made the light in the rest of the Studio seem soft and peaceful. To the left of the stage a larger table stood, holding bottles of spirits and glasses, with cases of beer and soft drinks underneath. The dozens of separate conversations filled the place with a restful, relaxed buzz that only ended slowly after the arrival of the meeting's organizers and the man who was to be the guest of honor for the night. As the general noise died down Boateng nodded at the three people now on the stage and said quietly, "Now, Doctor, you now I'm telling the truth, so don't interrupt. The woman up there is our leading writer. Don't ask me what she has written. I don't know and nobody cares. The white man on her left is her partner. He's the best photographer in this place for more than a hundred miles in all directions. Americano South African. The tall one I don't know, but he has the smile of a guy with foundation money. He's the reason we're here tonight, I think."

"Lawrence, let me make a suggestion. Why don't you just say who's who and what is what, and keep your comments for later?"

"You said that already." There was a lot of heat in the retort, but a few moments later she heard Boateng say very casually to Baako, "The woman in the middle, that is Akosua Russell. I thought you knew her."

"No," Baako said, "but I have heard of her. She edits *Kyerema*, doesn't she?"

"Sure, our own literary magazine. The country's most prestigious quarterly, trala."

"I haven't seen any recent issues, though."

"There aren't any," Boateng laughed. "Our quarterly comes out about once every two years."

"No funds?" Baako asked. But Boateng's only answer was to laugh in his face.

Up on the stage Akosua Russell whispered something to both of the men flanking her, making them break out with identical smiles a few moments apart, as if in leaning over to talk to each she had also given a strong ritual tug on some kind of smile string tying them together. Then she herself rose smiling like a queen at ease, waiting for silence before she spoke. Her speech was long, and most of it, from her first literary evening, was familiar to Juana. To make it pass more quickly she tried to think of the words as they would strike a person hearing them the first time in his life: what kind of meaning, she wondered, would Baako get from the long tale of efforts put into the development of an indigenous literature as well as an indigenous art, the two going inseparably, hand in hand? She looked now and then at Baako's face, but she saw nothing there now, neither hope nor nausea. When her speech was over, Akosua Russell introduced the evening's guest of honor. She seemed content to mention his name, Doctor Calvin Byrd, and to add that he was a man of great goodwill with a very strong and very healthy interest in the development of robust, indigenous art forms here. Doctor Calvin Byrd, judging from his smile and the slight nodding motion he made after these words, was happy with the introduction, and the gathering gave him its applause. Then Akosua Russell announced the bar was open for anybody who wanted drinks, part of the good work of Doctor Calvin Byrd — he smiled again — and Juana could see James Scalder rushing with happy speed toward the bar, hustling to keep his narrow lead over several young and eager men. Baako asked what Juana wanted to drink; she answered "Beer," and watched him move off to get it. Involuntarily her eyes caught the tall, slim figure of Akosua Russell. She seemed to be searching the small crowd, and in a moment she was in it, embracing people, kissing cheeks, whispering words in ears, then shifting off. Moving forward with quick grace, Akosua Russell cut a path through all the knots of people and came to stand directly in front of Lawrence Boateng. Putting a slim arm over his shoulder, she asked him, "Lawrence, you have a bit of your novel with you?"

"You know I carry it with me, in the car," Boateng said with some sullenness.

"Bring it," the woman said. "We'll have a reading." There was a smile on her lips, but it did not seem to have improved Boateng's humor.

"Who's the man, really?" His voice had a strong, hostile tinge.

"Bring your novel," Akosua Russell said. "We'll talk later. You come just after me." She winked at Boateng and was gone before he could say anything more.

"She's a crook!" he said, staring after her. But in a moment he was up and walking out into the car park.

On his way back with the drinks Baako waved to someone coming in from behind, and Juana thought it was Boateng returning with his manuscript, but when the man came over she saw it was the artist Ocran.

"I see you know each other," said Baako, offering Ocran a seat.

"Yes. Juana is the craziest optimist I've ever met," said Ocran.

"The last time we met, remember," she said, "you were swearing you'd never attend any more of these literary nights."

"Oh, I'm still disgusted," said Ocran. "I just came by out of idle curiosity."

"And I was thinking the really cynical had no curiosity at all," Juana laughed.

Ocran sighed and said, "Well, I suppose those little bits of hope stick to our old brains no matter what we see." He turned to Baako. "I didn't think I'd find you here."

"I wanted to take a look."

"You won't find anything, unfortunately."

"How do you know? After all —" Juana was saying, but Ocran cut her short.

"I know. You'll find some booze tonight, all right, if that is what you want. But as for art, that woman arranges these so-called soirées for only one thing: to get American money for her own use. Go ahead. Bring all your work and read it here. She'll tell the visiting Americans it was she who taught you to write. Or if that's too much she'll say she encouraged you, inspired you, anything, and she'll get more money to continue the good work. She's some sweet poison, that woman."

Boateng came back holding his manuscript and a lot of whisky in a beer glass. When Ocran asked if he would read tonight he hesitated, as though there was some uncertainty about the decision, then said yes.

"Akosua Russell should love you, letting her use your work the way she does," Ocran said. Boateng's lips tightened, but when he spoke it was to ask Ocran if he knew the other white man. Ocran said something out of which Juana could only catch a few words about money and con games. People left the bar singly and in small groups, holding bottles and glasses.

Up on the stage Akosua Russell whispered again to each of the two men beside her, rose to stand behind the table in the center, and waited for silence, striking a regal pose. All fell still.

"By request," she said slowly, at the same time placing a little book before her on the table with monumental poise, "I'll be reading my poem to start the soirée proper off."

"My poem?" Baako whispered.

"You heard right," Ocran replied.

"An epic poem," the voice on the stage declaimed. "The Coming of the Brilliant Light of the New Age to Amosema Junction Village'." Akosua Russell gazed out above the heads of the listeners, paused many seconds, then began.

> Say
> Say it
> Say it just this way
> Gently, gently,
> For this was how the maid,
> High-born princess of Amosema
> Brought light from a far, far land
> Unto her nighted village people.
> Say it
> Pastorally, pastorally
> Say.
>
> Say it
> Softly, softly say it.
> The maiden Ekua, royal, exquisite,
> Searched her mother's queendom for a mate
> And found none worthy
> For all said she was arrogant,
> This damsel walking with fairy grace,
> Traipsing, lilting, skipping,
> Pastorally, pastorally
> Say.
>
> Say it

Gingerly, gingerly, say
That one lucent dawn
Village maidens fetching snowy water
From pure gurgling spring streams,
Singing, playing in their normal ecstasy
Espied a handsome stranger from strange lands
On their happy, joyful way.
Say it
Bucolically, bucolically
Say.

Say it
Softly, softly, say
How the damsel Ekua's eyes
Went a sudden limpid blue with love,
How for three hours she and the stranger
Stood blushing in admiring amazement
And the beauteous earthen pot
Balanced on the maiden's virgin head
Rolled down and cracked
While at length the stranger said,
"Oh, thou!"
Lyrically, lyrically
Say.

Say it,
Blissfully, blissfully say.
For the stranger had shiny flaxen hair,
Limpid pools of blue for eyes,
The greatness of a thousand men,
Skin like purest shiny marble
Plus a dazzling chariot from beyond the seas.
And the damsel Ekua married him,
Blissfully, blissfully
Say.

Say it
Romantically, romantically say it.
The dynamic couple took the village,
Opened a retail store for magazines,
Taught letters to the children there,
Gave wholesome work to idle men,
Civilized the country entirely,

Reigning with new light o'er adoring subjects.
Say it
Pastorally, pastorally
Say.

Akosua Russell stood tall on the stage, smiling, quiet, composed, acknowledging applause.

"I keep thinking she'll have to vary this routine. Eight years back, when this place was opened, it was exactly like this." Ocran was shaking his head, looking up at the figure on the stage.

"Ah, but then colored lights played on her face while she read," Boateng said.

"Yes, I remember," answered Ocran. "It was a great success."

The voice from the stage came again: ". . . actually only started as the germ of a personal idea before it blossomed fully into poetry. A friend of mine has been calling it the most frequently anthologized West African poem. I drew up a partial list and came up with this:

"Two editions of the *British Council Treasury of Inspirational Colonial Poems*; three editions of the *British Council Treasury of Inspiring Commonwealth Poetry*; the *New Horizon Bards' Collection*; McConnery's *Epic Poems for Youthful Lands*, Schools Edition, and also Mrs. Gwendolyn Satterthwaite's *Longer Poems for Children*.

"But this is only one apect of the story. Some of you remember that I have turned the poem into an epic play first performed in this very theater on the Second National Arts and Crafts Day. I'm seriously considering developing it into a novel to be published abroad. Finally, Ghanavision plans to turn the poem first into a feature-length film, and then to adapt it for our TV."

There was more applause, and only when Akosua Russell raised her hand for quiet did it die down.

"If there are any questions now, I'll be glad to answer them," she said. She scanned the audience; a hand went up and she smiled and said, "Yes, you." A young man rose.

"My name is Adogboba," he said. "I'm from the north." He spoke with hesitation. "I'm a student waiting to go to the University and I want to write, er, I want to learn. I've been coming here for about three months now looking for the Workshop but I haven't been able to find a meeting. I wanted to say I'd like to join if you're still . . ." But Akosua Russell spoke just then and cut the young man off.

"That's really a question of normal routine," she said very evenly. "All such questions will be dealt with afterwards. See me after the soirée." From the audience there was a brief murmur. The student, looking utterly confused, swallowed the remainder of his words and sat, while Akosua Russell looked more intently over the heads of the audience and said, "If you have no more questions, we'll move on to item number two. Boateng, Lawrence Boateng, will read us a chapter from his novel awaitng publication. This is indeed a special treat, so let's give him a truly generous hand." And, leading the applause, Akosua Russell left the center of the stage and went back to her seat between the two white men.

Boateng rose, swayed slightly and walked toward the stage. He had his manuscript in his left hand, and in his right he was holding what remained of his tall whisky. For a moment Juana thought it possible he might fall: there was something weirdly centrifugal about his limbs as he got closer to the stage. Once there, he faced the audience, placed his manuscript on the table in front of him, raised the glass to his lips, drained the whisky, and just let the glass drop, shattering on the cement floor. Another murmur came from the audience, but then Akosua Russell caught everybody's eye by leaning to say something to the visitor and then slapping her thigh several times in boisterous laughter, and everyone relaxed. Juana wondered what would happen next, and watched closely as Boateng rustled the pages of his manuscript as though he had lost his place. After that he stood some time scrutinizing the audience like a searcher looking for a clue, then he began, "Before I read, I think . . ." he said, then paused, looking as if he had lost grasp of his own line of thought. The place fell quieter.

"I think that schoolboy said something important and you shut him up," he said at last in a rush of words. "Why? He wants to write, he can't find anyone. This is called a workshop and this boy can't come and learn, so what do you say to that?"

There was some commotion and Akosua Russell rose, making for the table, her lips working. But her words were inaudible; Boateng was shouting now, and in the general surprise everyone was listening to him: "Nobody meets to discuss real writing anymore. This has become a market where we're all sold. We're confused. There's money for this and that. Grants and so forth, but who swallows all this money? Everybody says it secretly, but I'm tired of secrets and whispers."

Akosua Russell had reached the speaker, but finding it impossible to shut him up, she was just standing looking unbelievingly at him; for the first time she looked vulnerable, even a little lost, and Juana was surprised to see how really old she could look.

In a moment Juana saw Billy Wells make a furious leap toward the center of the stage. She thought he would surely swing a fist at Boateng, but by the time he got to him his anger seemed to have cooled so that he only put an arm around him and tried to shove him gently off the stage. But in one swift and violent motion Boateng had disengaged himself and pushed Billy Wells hard against the table.

"Look, you Billy Wells," Boateng shouted in his fury, "you shouldn't be here anyhow. This is our studio, not your bedroom. Or are you now a writer too? You ran all the way from your America to come and be a writer in the country of the blind? Go 'way, man, don't touch me!"

But Billy Wells tried again to reach the angry man, and took such a sharp kick in the abdomen he gasped and bent with the pain. Two men ran up to the stage and took hold of Boateng. The audience began to break up, and in groups of two and three people began to leave. Akosua Russell and the American visitor had joined Billy Wells on the stage, and after several minutes of uncertain waiting the three left wordlessly. After them most of those remaining also went out, leaving the Studio deserted except for a little group that seemed involved in some long argument over in a corner by themselves, the men who had gone up to calm Lawrence Boateng, Boateng himself, the two men Juana had been sitting with, and the waiter putting away the glasses, the empty bottles and what was left of the drinks.

"I don't care," Boateng said, coming closer with the other two. "All of you will say I'm a drunkard. Say I'm mad, even. I've told the truth."

Ocran sighed and told him, "She won't forgive you, you know, and she hates hard."

"I had to speak," Boateng said quietly. "She's a blood-sucker."

"You allow her to be," said Ocran.

"What does that mean?"

"Why do you have to worry about her and how she gets her money? If you have something you want to do, don't waste your time with her. Do it."

"You think it's easy?" Boateng said, aggression coming back into his voice.

"Well," Ocran said, stretching out in the chair so that his legs stuck up awkwardly in front of him, "it isn't easy. An outburst like this, like this evening, is easier. But you won't do anything going on like this."

"So you too, you're on her side," Boateng said.

Ocran laughed. "She'd like to hear that. Look, Boateng, she's doing all the things you hate her for. But you could do better. You have a novel. O.K. You've had it done for six years, and you're waiting. Just waiting. A serious writer would have three, four more novels done by now, instead of waiting. And you'd have a totally different picture. Now all you're doing is adding your sand to the desert."

"She takes all the Foundation money . . ." Boateng started.

"That's what's wrong with you," said Ocran. "All you do is think of that bloody Foundation money first. Suppose it didn't exist? Look, your attacks on Akosua Russell are just stupid. All she's done is to find a way to make some money without working. She's no writer, and she knows it. She doesn't really care. She has the things she wants. If you want to compete with her and be a pimp, go ahead. But if you want to be serious, decide what your art is, and just go ahead with it. We aren't so full of energy, are we, so why waste so much of it fighting her? It's no waste to her; she does nothing anyhow."

Boateng made no answer. He just walked out alone, and in a minute the noisy exhaust of his car blasted the night outside. Ocran walked with Juana and Baako to the park, then drove off after saying good night.

"It's been exhausting, this night," Baako said.

"And cruel," Juana agreed. "You know, I'd like a ride. I feel depleted."

She noticed she was driving again, without much thought as to where she was going, along the Tema road. She said, "I'm also a creature of habit. Tend to drive out this way when I'm low."

"You're low now?" he asked her. His voice had a dejected flatness.

"Not too low," she answered. "But you, you sound . . . disappointed."

"I was looking," he said. "But there was nothing."

"I thought so."

"Yes, you were right. There isn't much you can find where I work, either."

"So you seem to have accepted that," she said.

"It's difficult. It's not really possible to work without others," he said.

"No." She thought of the professional, reassuring words she could have been saying; she would never be able to say them to him. "What Ocran said was true. But I wonder if you can all work in that kind of solitude."

There was no answer from Baako. She looked ahead through the windshield at the side of the road, lit by the headlights of her car. She saw his right hand reaching toward her. It hovered like a vague question and then touched her hair softly.

"We don't know each other," he said. "Yet sometimes I forget that."

"You know I work at Korle Bu."

"You're crazy."

She laughed too. "That was my way of telling you — if you're looking for sores to open, I have none."

"Lucky, then," he said. "But then you're supposed to cure people, not to have sores."

"I'll tell you as much as I can, then you mustn't ask for any more." He said nothing, and she wondered if he'd believe her. "I've been very sick before. Coming here was part of the cure. I don't know if it worked. But I was married. In love too. You know, I didn't need anyone else, then he left."

"How long?" he asked. "The marriage."

"Six." She cut across the road and parked the car on the grass, away from the side of the road, with the sand a few yards away. After locking the car she took Baako's hand and ran down to the sand, dragging him after her.

"You're surprised," she said, when he sat down on the sand beside her.

"It's not surprise," he said. "I like you." He was caressing her head again.

"Don't do that, though," she said.

"You don't like it?"

"When it's mechanical, no."

"It's not mechanical," he said, then, "I need to."

He stopped talking and for a long time just caressed her hair and her face. In the silence she felt very lonely. She took his hand and pressed it more firmly to her face, and the pressure calmed her. When she let go he moved his fingers down her neck and felt for her breasts, and in her own excitement she began to rub his back beneath his shirt. She let him reach down and run his fingers slowly in between her thighs till she felt ready, and then she raised her hips to help him slip off her underwear. She was momentarily surprised when he began loosening the buttons on her dress, but he laughed and said quite suddenly, "I hope you aren't pious or anything. It's a warm night."

"It's beautiful," she said.

When he too was naked he lay beside her on the sand and she could see the night light sharp on his face. He continued caressing the inside of her thighs and brought her left hand up to touch his own nipple. When he felt her wetness and came into her, his movement was diffident, and almost immediately he shook so that she was afraid he had already come. But he was holding her in a tense embrace, preventing her from moving, till he relaxed after a while and said, "It's a difficult thing, making love to someone I'm so strongly drawn to."

"It's easier with someone you don't feel strongly about?"

"The first time, yes, for me," he said. "When there's a lot of feeling I have to control myself, or I just rush out without waiting."

"O.K. now?" she said.

"Yes. That first rush is over."

He played with her hair, kissed her, always stopping and shifting his head so he could see her face in the moonlight. She did not feel him physically deep in her, and he was very light on her, so that the sand felt like a warm, firm cushion under her. Then she noticed his arms. "Relax. You won't crush me."

But he kept his weight off her. "The sand," he said, then seemed to have forgotten what he was talking about. He groped with his right hand, the index finger coming to rest against the knob of her clitoris, pushing softly against it and over it.

"I'll come too fast if you do that," she said.

"Good. Come. You can always come again," he said.

Yet she was not as quick as she had feared. She thought of his lightness, a ridiculous weight above her compared to Max's solid mass. She watched him, a little amused to see how carefully he moved, as if he thought he could bruise her going in and out. She pushed her hips up and felt him now deep against her. Now he was rubbing her, a bit too hard, so that she felt slightly sore. She reached for his hand, but before she could touch it all her control went out of her body, the salt taste of the air was deep in her throat, and she was saying words she'd thought she could never use again, and there was one moment when nothing that had happened to her made any difference, and all the steadying, controlling separatenesses between things did not matter at all to her. She could feel him come after her, and she held her body taut to keep him in longer, but after a while he got soft and she felt him wet against her hair before he turned and lay beside her also looking up into the sky, saying nothing.

"It was a horrible poem," he said so suddenly he startled her.

"Now why would you be thinking of that?" she asked him.

"It's the sea."

"What are you talking about, Baako?"

"It's one of our myths, you know," he said. "Mame Water and the Musician. She took the myth and tried her own variation on it."

"I'd say," she said. "What happens in the original?"

"The singer goes to the beach, playing his instrument. These days it's become a guitar. He's lonely, the singer, and he sings of that. So well a woman comes out of the sea, a very beautiful goddess, and they make love. She leaves him to go back to the sea, and they meet at long, fixed intervals only. It takes courage. The goddess is powerful, and the musician is filled with so much love he can't bear the separation. But then it is this separation itself which makes him sing as he has never sung before. Now he knows all there is to know about loneliness, about love, and power, and the fear that one night he'll go to the sea and Mame Water, that's the woman's name, will not be coming anymore. The singer is great, but he's also afraid, and after those nights on the shore, when the woman goes, there's no unhappier man on earth."

"It's an amazing story."

"The myths here are good," he said. "Only their use . . ." His voice died.

6 : Gyefo

BEYOND SENYA she kept going west till they saw ahead a half-hidden bay and decided to stop there. In silence both of them took off their clothes and got out wearing only their bathing things. She rolled up the windows without thinking very clearly of what she was doing and turned to find Baako walking slowly off, carrying in the crook of his right arm the green blanket from the trunk, the funny rainbow towel looking very big and soft around his neck, and also a magazine in his left hand. She hurried till she caught up with him and said, "You won't be reading that, Baako." He replied as if she had said something extremely solemn.

"I was bringing it for both of us."

"You plan for us to need it?" She reached out with a finger and touched him in the side where his ribs showed a little, but this time he did not break down with his ticklish laughter; he did not even begin to laugh, but looked at her with a steady look that remained above a momentary, uneasy smile.

"Is anything the matter?" she asked.

"No," he answered immediately. "Why?"

"You look, I don't know, preoccupied."

In a place of an answer he rolled up the magazine and stuck it in the space between his right armpit and the blanket, then held out his left hand and took her right in a tight, needy grasp. He let go of her hand to spread out the blanket on the sand when they reached the shore of the bay. She lay with her back on the blanket watching him while he stood covering the sun with his body, looking away, unable to make up his mind about something that had troubled him a long time, perhaps. She felt the heat of the sand below coming up to her through the thickness of the blanket; almost at the same time he shifted and the sun came into her open eyes in needles of light that continued to hurt after she had shut her eyelids against them. She turned over and felt the heat more comforting against her belly and her thighs. When she opened her eyes she saw the magazine on the blanket to her left. The piece of it that had escaped Baako's shadow glared unpleasantly, and it was she who took it and placed it open and folded so that her head was between the sun and the page that showed, and the glare was killed. Still Baako made no comment about her being the one to begin reading. He sat beside her, and after a while she felt the touch of his fingers on the back of her right thigh, just beneath her bathing suit. The touch made her think of a blind person's feeling hands. It was slow, going down her leg till the reaching fingers came to the sole and the gentle downward slide of their nails produced in her an involuntary half-shiver before the fingers began again. She felt too warm all over. Baako's fingers began to move with too much ease, as though they were now slipping over sweat starting to come up. He too must have felt something of the sort; he stopped stroking her thigh and lay down beside her. She could see his face, but did not turn to look at him directly until he quietly raised his head and kissed her neck, caressing and sucking it so long he was beginning to hurt her and she had to push him away.

"You hurt me just then," she said.

"Sorry. I didn't mean to."

"I'm hot." An immense feeling of laziness was in her, and she closed her eyes and turned on her back, wishing the afternoon did not have a sun with so much strength in it. She heard his voice.

"Come."

She opened her eyes and saw him, smiling now, and holding out a hand to her. She gave him her hand and he pulled her up and onto the sand. The heat burned her sole with every step, so she was glad when he started running and pulling her after him toward the surf. For yards and yards the water only came up to their knees, then abruptly both of them fell in a trough that brought the water up to her neck in a swell, and when they climbed out on the other side the water was level with her breasts.

"What was bothering you?" she asked again.

"Nothing," he said. "Nothing in particular."

She could see his interest was not in the words he had been saying. His hands were searching for her again, touching her, closing and opening in movements that often seemed to escape his control.

"I was trying," he said, in a voice unexpectedly free of tension, "to get hold of something. It was like a growing happiness, or the beginning of a good understanding which would vanish easily in a moment. Have you never felt like that?"

"Maybe," she answered. "I don't know exactly what you mean."

They had waded a long way past the white of breaking surf. The waves passing them were blue-green turning metallic colors where sunlight glided in the water's thousands of little hollows. At long intervals a giant swell lifted both of them and took them suspended a way back in the direction of the beach before their feet found bottom again.

"Did you succeed in keeping it in, not letting it go?" she asked.

"It slipped off again," he shook his head. "Then I stopped trying."

He was stroking her again, round her neck and down her back. His touch was not hard, yet it had a possessiveness to it that made her feel he was reaching for her the way he might have done a replacement he had found for the understanding which had just now eluded him. She brought her hands together, palm to palm, and holding the fingers outward ran their tips slowly down his head, forehead, nose, mouth, chin till they slipped down his neck and chest and fell in the water, making a feeble sound.

"Very Catholic," he said.

She laughed. She too had seen the readiness with which her hands made the prayer clasp, but she would have preferred to let her thoughts wander elsewhere. The only time she had asked him, he had told her he had been a kind of pagan all his life, and then he had laughed at her for saying she herself was an atheist. "You don't act that way," he had said. "I think you're a Catholic or, better still, a pagan." He had offered no explanation, but thinking about the words she had found an awkward truth about herself. She had had to admit she was concerned with salvation still, though she permitted herself the veil of other names. Too much of her lay outside of herself, that was the trouble. Like some forest woman whose gods were in all the trees and hills and people around her, the meaning of her life remained in her defeated attempts to purify her environment, right down to the final, futile decision to try to salvage discrete individuals in the general carnage. Sometimes she could almost understand the salutary cynicism of Protestants, their ability to kill all empathy, to pull in all wandering bits of self into the one self, trying for an isolated heaven in the shrinking flight inward. She could almost understand it, but even if there were some ultimate peace in it, it would never reach her to change her from within.

He stopped her thinking with his searching fingers. They tried caressing a nipple through wet cloth but seemed to find only the entire breast at once. Baako held her close and reached behind her, unfastening the single button, then slipping a hand up the loose front to take her nipple and rub it between thumb and index finger.

"Not that," she said, "not here."

"Why not?" She turned to look toward the shore, heard his laughter behind her and words, "All Accra suddenly coming and looking . . ." Before she could turn again a strong wave had caught her and struggling to balance herself she felt the loose bra slip away down her arms stretched out in the water. The wave passed and the breeze felt cool over her naked breasts. Behind her Baako was still laughing a laugh which stopped then began again when she turned and for the first time he saw the bra was gone. He looked out after the wave. It had broken now and was getting sucked back into the body of the sea.

"It's going to float up soon," he said.

But the bra did not appear and to put him out of his confusion she smiled at him and said, "It doesn't matter. We can find it later."

He bent to reach her breasts with his mouth, taking the same nipple in a kiss and sucking on it so that the pleasure did not quite begin to hurt; then he let go and sank beneath the water and in a moment she felt him trying to take down the trunks also and she helped him. He rose with them behind her and came back round only after he had slipped them over his head, leaving them hanging round his neck along his back. Just as he began again to suck the nipple she asked what he had done himself, and for an answer he just held her right hand and took it down so she could touch his trunks. He had tied the string around his left knee.

She felt him run his fingers down the small of her back till they came to the end of her spine and he slid them farther down where they lingered, caressing her buttocks, squeezing them and going flat against them. She brought her right hand up his thigh and found him hard already. Looking at the water she thought it funny how impossible it now was for her to tell whether her feeling of readiness was true or not. In the water there was something like a dryness that made it hard at first for him to come into her, and then when he was in she turned too wet with incoming seawater that made him feel softly abrasive trying to move in her. Then without a word he lifted her and guided her legs behind him and around, and when he held her there she could feel him now warm in back of her.

"I'm heavy," she said.

"Not in water."

"Oh, thanks." She drew back slightly, laughed at his pained surprise, then pressed herself back; but the water that felt warm on her outer skin gave her a strange, rather unpleasant feeling within now. When she stopped Baako pulled her hard against himself and then began to move her from side to side, and she felt pleasure again.

"It's not . . . intense, it's strange," she said.

"You never made love in the sea?"

"No," she said. "But I like it now. I feel like going on and on."

She was surprised when he moved his left hand and in a swift movement pushed a finger deep up in her arse, but the unpleasant feeling was momentary; in its place rose a sensation of queerly heightened sweetness as she felt the membrane inside her caught between Baako's finger and penis; he turned the finger round toward her back, groping in a soft reach for the base of her spine, and that was when she came — a long coming so complete that she felt her head go beneath the water but did not care, and it was Baako who held her head and brought it up again. She held him hard till she could feel his juice enter her, made tepid by the cooler water, and then he stood holding her, quite still.

"You've done it very often?" she asked him.

"What?"

"Made love in the sea. You said you had."

"No," he said. "I was asking you."

"This wasn't the first time for you."

"Maybe not," he said without much interest. Then, "Here we're supposed to do it all when we're born, anyway. The first swim and the first fuck. There's a saying there's no way you can get out of your mother without."

"You made that up." She swam lazily away on her back, then turned. Baako had been saying something to her.

"I didn't hear you," she said when her feet touched bottom.

"I'm getting cold," he said.

"Get under the water."

He dived under noisily and in a second she felt him grab her by the leg, then move a teasing finger up between her thighs. She tried to hold the hand and shouted no, but Baako was still beneath the water and the hand had come to a stop before he rose wet and laughing.

"Don't do that, Baako, it hurts now," she said. He stopped.

"Jesus, my back hurts. Let's go back, Juana."

She felt embarrassed at first, but she saw him laughing at her, turning all round and cupping his right hand to his ear. She was running to catch up with him on the dry sand when without warning he lay down and began to roll over and over.

"You're crazy. You'll get all sandy!" she shouted after him. But he shouted back: "Try it. It's the best way to get dry. The sand won't stick."

She got a gentle burning feel from the sand beneath her; the first hot grains stuck to her but fell off as she rolled the opposite way from Baako, leaving her body in a few minutes baked and free, and only her hair still moist from the sea.

They walked back up where the blanket was. She lay forward on it, already halfway lost in sleep, while Baako sat staring once more into the sea. When she opened her eyes again he was looking at her.

"I don't think we'll be alone very much longer now," he said.

"Why?" She sat up.

"Look."

Where he was pointing she could see nothing but a lone sea gull suspended on its wings high in the sky above the water.

"It's only a sea gull, just one," she said. Just then the bird folded its wings and dropped in a steep ball down into the sea; and almost before it had touched water it was up again, flying eastward, silent and fast and low now.

"She caught it," Baako said calmly, and looking after the circling bird Juana saw a brief, small flash of light near its head, tried to see what it was but got in her eyes a strong ray of sunlight coming off the rolled-up window of her car up the way and turned her look back down against the blanket's dullness. Two more gulls came to join the first, followed by barely audible voices from beyond the bay that quickly became a series of shouts from a hidden crowd. A small canoe came toward the beach, carrying no more than nine men all naked down to the waist save one who had on a coat on top of his calico pants. Juana took the rainbow towel from Baako, made a fuck-you sign to him when she saw he was smiling, and covered herself with the towel. By the time the canoe reached the shore a crowd much larger than the group that had come in it had arrived on the bay beach, waiting with pans and large, round wooden trays on their heads for the coming fishermen. The fishermen had brought the ends of two ropes with them. Around these, two groups of men, from those who had come walking, formed and moved apart, and then began pulling in the ropes.

It was a confused movement of men around taut ropes Juana saw at first; she looked at Baako thinking to ask him for some short explanation of the scene before her, but his look silenced her. He looked lost in what he was seeing, like a man on the point of finding something he has grasped and lost and fears he will lose again any moment. He looked with no love at all, at first. Juana saw emotion in his face, but it was fear, something close to hate, an awed suspicion, and she wondered if it was possible he was seeing all this for the first time in his life. She knew if would be useless to ask him anything now, so she too watched.

Both groups of men went up beyond the sand and there tied the ends of their ropes around the trunks of coconut trees. After that they rushed down to the sea and dragged more rope back with them toward the anchoring trees, making slow snaking piles beneath them. A boy rushed enthusiastically down and back twice with them, but the third time up he got in the way of a huge, towering man who knocked him sideways flat into the sand. The boy rose scratching his head as if what had happened had just now made him lose certainty of his place in life. The men went down again after more rope and this time he did not follow them. Instead he went to the closer of the coconut trees and sat under it, beside the growing pile of rope. He turned his head upward, uncertainly, then seemed to have found what he was looking for. The men came back pulling on the rope with a casual hostility. Juana looked again at Baako; his eyes were fixed upon the legs and arms of these men: legs and thighs bulging with too much packed-in power, arms filled with rigid muscle, moving all at once in too many undecided directions. It was very much like fear, the look in Baako's eyes.

Soft wood on metal gave an echoing treble womansound, then died quetly. Before Juana looked in the boy's direction again she saw

Baako turn too and with the turn his face began to grow peaceful and relaxed.

The boy had found a double gong. He struck it again and this time the sound was hoarse and deep. Making tentative noises, he struck alternate deep and high notes; in a while what sounded at first like his playful sounds had taken on a definite rhythm, and he kept it up. The men came with their rope, sweating, and each time took little notice of the boy. But they were now quieter, and some seemed a bit tired already, so that they were taking more time going down to the sea and back, moving into a clearer pace. Then in a gap of quiet when neither the breeze nor the men's voices were high, the small boy added his voice to the beating of his gong. It was a clear voice, high as a woman's, and the song it was carrying could have been anything about the sea, like a woman's long lament for one more drowned fisherman. One irritated strong man kicked sand at the boy and shouted at him, perhaps to shut him up; he stopped his singing only briefly, recovered and continued. On the next return another big-bodied man, this one with a slow, pensive step, one of those who had reached the bay in the canoe, took up the song, his voice deeper but his rhythm the same. Where the two singers paused the only refrain was the sound of the sea, till one after the other the remaining men and a few of the waiting women began also to hum endings to the song. Now the pulling took a rhythm from the general song. The men dug their feet deep into the sand and pulled from fixed positions on the rope.

It was two hours at least before the bag net itself emerged from the water, but time passed quickly, imperceptibly, and the sun mellowed to an early evening warmth. In that time the boy started seven separate songs, each in itself made up of long subtly changing verses held over easy chorus hums, and the men sometimes unfixed themselves and pulled on the ropes with a slow shuffling march whose steps were all measured to the songs. And then it broke.

The gulls grew into dozens. The bag net, vaginal and black, came sliding heavy up the beach on a long wave. Juana heard from that distance the soft and steady sound made by the beating flesh of still-living fish trapped now in their final desperation. There was no one heeding songs now. The men's muscles suddenly regained their swollen, knotted shapes from before and rushed disordered at the net. Behind them the boy still sang, softly, not in any public way, but to himself, though occasionally a sharp cry, resembling an uncontrollable complaint, broke the near-silent softness of whatever he had left to sing. Women went forward with their trays for fish, and their money. The men left their beached canoe and piled thick ropes on their strong backs to walk where the larger crowd had come from. The boy went last, looking in the sand for still useful bits of unsold fish, perhaps, but he found none. He was also going back along the curve of the bay when he stooped suddenly by the water and when he stood upright again Juana saw in his hands the missing bra she had left in the sea.

"Did you see that, Baako?"

"He found your bra," he answered. 'I'll get it." He rose to go after the boy, but Juana held him back. The boy wrapped the strange garment he had found about his head; his voice died before he too disappeared.

Going back, she drove a long way before breaking the silence.

"You had eyes only for that little boy," she said.

"I thought you saw it too."

"Saw what?"

"That boy, he was giving those men something they didn't have."

"They pushed him around pretty badly, I'd say."

"Yes, they did." He was quiet a long time, staring out the window into the rushing bush and grass. Then turning to look at her, he smiled with some inner pleasure and told her, "The electric grid should be finished next month."

"Where did you hear that?" she asked him.

"We had a production meeting."

"One month here seems to mean five years," she said, and it disturbed her that he didn't even smile.

"It'll be good to see sets actually in the villages."

"They'll be waiting centuries, more likely, I'm afraid," she said. "Baako, you expect too much."

"What do you want me to do?" Unable to find words, she took her eyes off the road long enough to kiss him lightly on the cheek. "I still don't know what you think I should do," he insisted.

"I was just hoping, among other things . . ." she was doing her best not to sound apologetic, "that you won't tie your happiness too closely to what happens, what other people do or say."

He did not push her to answer any more questions, and she felt relieved. Behind them the sun had dropped below the horizon; coming down a hill she caught a brief glimpse of the city ahead of her, its lights already on. She hoped she had not driven him from her now, but there was no telling. He looked out the window most of the time, but once he stared at her so long and with so much concentration, like a person taking a farewell look, that even in the falling darkness she could not turn to look back at him. She just drove faster.

7 : Igya

IT WAS A MIRAGE after all — the peace he'd thought would follow after his resignation. He'd been looking forward to a quiet time in which he'd calmly think his way outward into something not so empty. The time had come but instead of peace it had brought a whirling torture to fill his mind as he tried in vain to grasp some substance out of the blighted year behind. There was a clear, insistent certainty, but it lay with the past, with the uselessness he had found in that direction, the essential wasteful absurdity of it. When he tried to focus on some way out, the dance of memories turned into a wild, prolific multitude of leaping thoughts and leaping images that left not a moment's space for a different wish but drew him impotently back into the unending waste, the stupid stream against which he was powerless even to set his own mind.

It was senseless, that much was clear. But this was a clarity with a dangerous giddy quality he would have to watch. Because there were all the others. They could not help but see the things he'd seen and more. But they accepted it, went through the myriad motions anyone could see were empty, and were going about with this amazing happy kind of intent to build up whole structures filled with thousands doing nothing but finding the most puffed-up pompous ways, strutting around a land of paupers offering extravagance as the universal guide. At times it had seemed too much like a garish nightmare played out in the brief glare of strong lights, something really impossible. But there it was all the time, happening as though in life the games played in children's schools had never found a way to end, except that some of the posts marking corners and goals had been pulled out and lost, and there was nothing to choose between different hordes of grandly reeling runners with nowhere to go. At work the engineers wore white-white or suits and sat balancing phones behind new furniture and grew utterly perplexed if some machine broke down and had to be fixed. The producers seldom worked at night but the names and titles they had had put on their doors and desks were done in paint that glowed against the dark. The way they understood their work, it was more travel than production. All had been abroad, to different countries overseas for training, and had brought back fond footage of themselves visiting foreign studios, seeing strange sights and eating extraordinary foods in famous places. To fill program space and time they took routine trips to all the embassies in town to ask for films and tapes to be run on the television screen after the opening music and credit titles. At intervals there was a change: something that was happening anyway was televised, like some poetry reading caught with fixed cameras. He tried to push down one grisly thought, but it was slippery and it rose: a script on slavery had been done, accepted, approved, stamped and routinely filed. It would have gotten lost unused, except that the Scalder woman saw it, said she liked it and decided to turn it into theater. There was a white man in the script, the enslaver, helped by a bloated African chieftain and his trinket-wearing court of parasites. In the Scalder woman's play the white man disappeared, to be replaced by a brutish whip-swinging African, and the whole thing became purely a free-for-all among yelling tribal savages. It was duly filmed for Ghanavision.

He tried to shift away from it but the thought stayed suspended in his brain, turning and moving in its own slow, heavy time. At one point he'd had some hope, thinking maybe at Ghanavision he'd found more of this stagnancy than was normal. But later he had gone up and down, across the land with Juana, and he'd seen the same sterility riding on top of everything, destroying hope in all who lived under it. He'd got a first sense of that destruction of worth from Gariba, the one producer who could surprise him with the beauty of some conception of his. Baako had come to hate him; at first he'd only felt irritated by the sidelong manner in which Gariba seemed to present everything, but then the irritation had deepened into a kind of contempt when he understood Gariba was constantly trying to tell him something, to indicate he knew the sterility had caught him, and that his answer to the trap was a necessary acceptance. Gariba was always drawing back before he'd said enough to make full sense, except once when he'd talked laughingly, calling himself a potentially good producer who'd learned not to insist on being productive. He'd told it as a wild joke, and he'd seemed happy telling it: a long, easy string of little anecdotes about his arrival in Accra, the eagerness with which he'd done simple, didactic scripts, and the initial surprise when he noticed every production meeting ended with the Director saying there was no film, no tape.

"Why the shortage?" Baako had asked, and Gariba's hidden smile had semed quite unnecessary then.

"You'll see. We have to follow the Head of State and try to get pretty pictures of him and those around him. Isn't that difficult? We had a lecture before you came. A nation is built through glorifying its big shots. That's our job, anyway."

Something characteristic had happened then. The joking tone got swallowed into Gariba's usual quiet resignation, and there was no pursuing what he'd just said, and Baako had been filled with a strange, frustrated anger. That was the first time he'd found himself walking over to Juana's place. He hadn't intended to, and if he had thought of it the thought of her not being home yet would have made him turn back. But he walked as surely as if he'd been meaning to all along, a desire for contact with something he loved growing keen and terrible in him, as if his person would simply explode if he didn't go. He began, then gave up wondering what would have happened to his and Juana's love without the emptiness around pushing them closer.

He had seen the ends of the country with her and the feeling between them had grown and deepened itself with the most natural ease. The brown roadbeds up north with their dangerous gravelly sides and laterite dust had remained beautiful in his mind, and the villages on the way down from Tumu and Wa were now sounds, though there was no forgetting them as places where maimed people and sickness walked down every half-hidden path, where he'd come to understand finally that Juana not only saw the pain, but felt it in herself and was holding down something straining to scream out from within her own body. Sibele Lilixia Jefiso Han Sabuli Fran Naro Jang Kaleo Pirisi and Wa.

Then Tanina Ga Kulmasa Gindabo Tuna Nakwaby Sawla Mankuma; Bole Lampurga Seripe Tinga Yidala Teselima before the other ferry over the river Volta at Bamboi, there a thin rope of water, light brown with mud and strangely dry. There was no remembering precisely where, between which two names he had stared at Juana's face as she drove, felt the threatening disappointment there and surprised her with a sudden question: "You're unhappy."

He'd watched her wait a while then turn the rearview mirror on its hinge so she could see her face before she answered, straining a little to see the whole of her face, "I don't look any unhappier than you."

"I didn't say you look. You are."

She'd made no attempt to give him an answer. He knew she was trying to make him forget the question, taking his hand in hers and caressing it with an intensity that begged him to move on to something else.

"Why?" He would persist until she broke her silence. He did not take his eyes off her face, so that when she turned to see if he was still waiting for her answer the sight of him staring so directly into her eyes seemed to produce a gentle surprise.

"It was all like the Chief Engineer at the other ferry, at Yeji," she said. "The doctors here know things are a mess. But they accept it. Like some hopeless reality they can't even think of changing, except to make the usual special arrangements for Senior Officers, friends, what have you. They told me I was wasting my time talking of a changed approach. A couple of them got very hostile and said I was wasting *their* time. Just like at the ferry."

The drive north from Kumasi to that ferry had been tiring. It was a little after three when Juana drove by the food and drink shacks lining the approach road and brought the car to the river. An escort policeman directed her to a stop behind two other cars, and she got out yawning, stretching her whole body and saying, "I'm so hungry."

"There's food back there."

"Yes," she answered. "I saw some fufu. The cocoyam made me homesick."

He went with her to stand in line and had to tease a driver out ahead to keep him from offering them his place, then stood relaxed, taking in the talk of the women pounding fufu and the waiting men.

"This stranger is actually coming to eat pepper too."

"Speak softly. Her husband understands."

"No need to whisper. Who has insulted her?"

"Besides, I swear they're not married."

"They are."

"The way they came, there's so much love between them they can't be married."

"That's you again, Yaa Anoa. Your marriage has really soured your mouth."

When they'd eaten they walked alongside the swollen river, looking at the people and the water. Close to the ferry landing they came upon a naked madman, tall and thin, gazing over the expanse as if he had a power to see the bank beyond the horizon, then staring hard into the water at his feet. He was talking, and he too spoke Twi.

"What's he saying?" Juana asked.

"Something about the water." He drew her closer to the madman and heard the voice more clearly. "He says it's beneath the water. Everything. The sky. Anyone who looks deep can see it. Down below the water."

"He's saying something else," she said.

"No. Just repeating and changing the same thing."

A deep horn sounded one long blast from across the river. The madman turned irritably away from the direction of the sound and then, as if it meant some unforgettable personal harm to him, wailed out a long stream of curses against the coming boat. The ferryboat itself appeared in full view, turning straight after a mangrove screen in the water. It was painted yellow and white, and now and then when it rose softly a few inches above the water's swell, its painted sloping bottom showed a clear red. Above the vehicles the people crossing stood in packed crowds on the platforms on either side of the boat, many of them waving to the bank, as though they were now going, not coming. The ferry glided peacefully, in a great silence, toward the landing jetty.

On land the ferry's arrival shattered the existing quiet. Drivers laughed and shouted, leaped into their trucks and lorries, shifted out of old places in the confused line and drove in a humming, vibrating stampede toward the water. A lorry loaded to its roof with plantain and cassava nosed forward till its front fender nudged the back of the last government bus and its driver stopped it and leaped out.

"Hey, Skido!" another driver shouted, "you wan' pass me?"

Turning to face the driver who'd shouted after him, Skido looked very small. He had quick eyes and he seemed constantly to be working his face into a look of unfrightened determination. It seemed also that he was never very far from tears.

"I was here long before you," Skido said. There had been a note of entreaty in his voice, but the last words had a snapping, angry tone. "I've waited three days by the river and it's food I have in my lorry, not iron. I won't let it happen again."

"We'll see," the other driver said, walking calmly away.

The ferryboat had reached the bank. The noise of ready vehicle engines absorbed all other sound save the heavier, steadier throbbing of the ferryboat engine itself. Baako got into the car behind the wheel, took out the ferry tickets and gave them to Juana to hold. Ahead of the waiting traffic the same escort policeman directed arriving cars and buses and lorries onto land after the passengers had streamed down to the jetty and the bank. The policeman then moved to the center of the road. He waved one government bus forward to the jetty, then a second. As the third bus rolled forward, the hum of the other traffic waiting to be beckoned forward took on a kind of sullen strength and the air was charged with an unsteady power, rising on the noise like something about to slip loose, out of control, at any moment. After the last government bus the policeman took three steps out of the middle of the road, moving left toward the parked cars and gesturing to the driver of the first in line to come forward. That same instant a truck bore down powerfully from far behind, roared in a sharp turn that brought it into the space just vacated by the policeman, and with its speed unchecked made it onto the ferry. The policeman turned, his mouth open and shaped for some angry sound; the words were swallowed in the huge roar of a reckless line of other trucks and lorries crashing after and into each other, arriving singly out of the utter chaos somehow undestroyed on the heaving boat. In the confusion an anguished shout cut through all the thick noise, riding it on a higher pitch: "Christ!"

The man called Skido was running to his lorry, but the stream of heavy machines blocked his path, and six trucks went past him before he made a crazy dash in front of the seventh and took a flying jump into his seat, starting his lorry almost in that same movement.

Closer by, the owners of the two cars in front had caught the policeman in a hot argument, gesticulating at him and getting gestures of his helplessness in reply.

Skido's lorry shot forward with a sudden sound like a wounded animal and looking ahead of it Baako felt a hot dryness in his brain and then he heard Juana's voice like an echo from within himself.

"But there's no space!" and she was clutching his hand. He held her, saying nothing, watching the frantic lorry on the jetty. It went relentlessly forward, struggling for inches of tail space left on the ferry platform. Now the human silence was again broken, the shouts a wild mixture of astonishment, fear, hate, perhaps even admiration for this driver gone crazy.

The ferry horn blew a deep bass note. Skido edged his lorry forward till the truck ahead stopped its movement. He stuck head and shoulders out and screamed something at a man beside him on the ferry; the man was the same big-muscled driver who had shouted at Skido when the boat had come. Now he shook all over with brief laughter, but otherwise did not make one move. Skido backed his lorry, then braked. Instead of reversing clear off the ramp he just revved the engine to a sickening screech and crashed strongly forward into the rear of the big man's truck. It moved forward a bit and Skido's lorry took the extra space. But still the back half of the lorry was left on the land jetty. Another long horn blast sounded and the boat gave a slow, powerful shudder.

"They won't move like that," Juana was saying, "they won't move."

The ferryboat began to move from the jetty. It was slow. Skido's lorry stood a long, suspended moment with its rear tires on land and its front on the moving boat. Then it seemed to roll forward slightly as the boat gathered speed, and the tail end of it cleared the land and dangled there in the air at the high end of the ferry boat. It took only a few seconds, but it was a long silence in which the driver Skido tried to jump free of his lorry. He jumped, but immediately he fell in the ferry's wake just as the lorry itself slipped backward and quietly flipped all the way on its back as it hit the water and was sucked under with its tight-packed load. Something like a wave rose then from the hollow the lorry made, followed moments after by huge bubbles chasing each other up to the surface, then smaller, slower ones and near the very end a long, thin finger of blood that floated out of the shaken water and began spreading in a wild leaf pattern losing its red, getting brown away from the center.

Two men had jumped into the water after Skido and his lorry. They dived when they reached the center of the still expanding ripples, and twice came up for air. The third time the first led the second down and after another long silence both came up without Skido and swam to the bank.

Baako said: "Let's go."

"Where?" Juana asked.

"Back through the town. I wonder who's in charge of this."

He turned the car round. A wind lifted off the river and blew through the women's headkerchiefs and cover cloths, giving the whispering knots of people an awed, lost air. He drove carefully back along the approach road and at the entrance asked the policeman where the big man lived. In the direction the policeman had pointed they came to a sign that said:

PUBLIC WORKS DEPARTMENT

ENGINEER'S RESIDENCE

The drivers of the other cars had followed them, and the engineer welcomed them all into his sitting room, motioned to them to sit down and sank back down into a large sofa. The one who had argued most heatedly with the escort policeman at the ferry was the first to speak.

"There's been an accident at the river," he said solemnly.

"Oh yes?" the engineer asked, adding calmly, "The fools."

"It's serious," Baako cut in.

"Of course, of course," the engineer said. He stared carefully at a crease in his starched white shorts, then slowly flicked at something, a loose end of thread or a floating speck. "It's always serious. They're just like animals. They don't think, that's all."

At this point an escort policeman, the same one who'd been at the ferry, knocked at the open door and remained at attention outside it till the engineer ordered him to enter.

"Accident to report, sah!" the escort said.

"Yes, Idrissu, what is it?"

"River entry block again. Lorry sah."

"Good," said the engineer. "We'll have it cleared tomorrow."

"Man die, sah."

"Oh?"

"Man die, sah."

"All right, Idrissu. Dismiss."

The policeman gave a salute and went out. Baako rose, reaching for Juana's hand.

"Sit down, sit down," the engineer said.

"I thought we were going down," Baako said.

"Going down? Down where?" the engineer asked.

"To the river. The dead man . . ."

"Ah, the dead man." The engineer relaxed as Baako sat down again. "Nothing to be done now. I have to send for a caterpillar.

Tomorrow the river can be cleared and the body will go to Kumasi for a postmortem. Nothing we can do now."

"But we should . . ."

The engineer ignored his words, looking at everyone there in turn. "You should have come to see me directly in the first place. You wouldn't have been caught in this mess. I'm going to give you special chits. Priority. Tomorrow the escort will be under strict orders to put you on first."

Baako realized he'd been staring straight at the engineer, and that he was now staring back.

"It could have been prevented," he said.

"What could have been prevented?" the engineer asked him with an irritated smile.

"The accident," he said.

"How?"

"It's the openness of the approach that makes the drivers rush. If the approach could be tarred and made to take only one vehicle at a time . . ."

"No one asks them to rush. If they don't make the last ferry at four they can wait till morning."

"They lose a day."

"That's right, they lose a day," the engineer said.

"I think," said Baako, "the man who died said he'd waited three days already."

"A bit more patience and he'd still be alive. Why are they in such a hurry anyway?"

"This one was carrying food up north," Baako said. A restless silence followed. "Is a day and night service impossible? There's more than enough traffic."

"We have three oil deliveries a week. Enough for the boat to run from six to five," the engineer said firmly.

"Did you decide that?" Baako asked.

"General operational rules."

"But they make no sense. Surely you've got the power to change them?"

The engineer was looking at him, working his throat as though something abrasive had gotten stuck to his adam's apple and he needed to swallow hard to get rid of it. "Look, friend," he said in the silence, "I met two young men just like you. Talking easily, knowing my job better than myself. Listen: I joined the PWD twenty-three whole years ago. I was patient, and waited, that's why I have my present post." He rose, and the others got up too. "How many cars, four?"

"Three," one of the men answered.

The engineer signed three chits with the words SPECIAL PRIORITY stamped on them. He gave the two men theirs and held out the third to Baako, looking into his eyes and adding, "You know one sure way of avoiding the mess. Why don't you fly?"

The other two laughed nervously all the way to the rest house.

Inside the rest house, a cool night breeze came through the gauze-covered windows. A steward came to ask, "What time massa an' madam wan' wake up? I go come call am."

Baako gave him a weak answer. "Thanks, man, but don't come and call us. We'll get up by ourselves." The steward looked puzzled, said good night and went out silently, like a ghost.

When they went to the bathroom Juana undressed first and stepped under the shower, letting it run slowly, waiting. Baako stood leaning against the door and watched her, unable for a while to make up his mind about the little routine actions he should take. Taking off his clothes, he could not stop his mind from spinning off after strange, uncalled-for memories that made him forget this moment and this place, except for the softly moving form of Juana under the falling water.

"Baako."

The water put a vibration in her voice, a good sound that brought his focus back to her and the shower.

"Baako, come under, come with me."

He took breath as she turned on a stronger stream and moved sideways herself so he could get the full force of descending water. He brought her back under, holding her close to himself a long, silent time, then he stepped back and lost himself in the look of her body. He let her soap his hair and his whole body, then he washed off the foam and bent and touched her with both hands, moving his fingers gently up her body, feeling the wet smoothness of her flesh, and when he reached her neck he pressed her closer and kissed her lightly there before reaching for the towels, giving one to her.

A scent, soft and clear, of ripening mangoes and fine dust before rain came with the breeze through the gauze windows, and in the bed the damp rest house sheets felt warm and comforting to the skin.

Neither of them slept. He could hear her breathing; it was soft and easy, but at intervals a long breath broke through and her touch on his arm under the top sheet grew momentarily firmer. He lay looking at the ceiling, at a spot where the turned-down flame of the hurricane lamp made a pattern, like a spider's web, of black shadows and dark, orange light. He felt warm sweat slide down his back. Juana's breathing was more audible now, and even, a sleeper's breathing.

Baako got up and put his clothes back on, making no noise. A drizzle, more heavy mist than rain, had begun outside. He walked in the softening dust beneath the mango trees and turned right when he came to the road, going in the direction of the river. He walked slowly, the drizzle touching his face in a fine spray. Along his back the initial warmth of the seat had turned cool.

A half mile off he saw dozens of oil-lamp flames burning with little restless motions directly against the drizzle. Footsteps sounded to one side behind him, and turning, he saw it was Juana. He took her hand and went with her toward the lights and the dark river.

The riverside in the night was changed completely from what it had been in the daylight. The screeching rush was gone, together with the curses of sweating, angry men. A heavy breeze rose off the water, turning the misty drizzle into a fine sporadic spray and finally blowing out the little oil lamps one after the other. There were several people, but there was no noise, except now and then a short word, a request or a reply, coming from one of the men. There were seven or eight men, drivers and their mates, moving their lorries back up the approach road, making room by the jetty. They had positioned one lorry so its headlamps lit the bank and the river, the light reaching beyond the point where Skido had fallen beneath his vehicle.

Close by, out of the silence, a voice choking with irritation shouted, "Big man, stand back!" As he moved out of the way Baako couldn't let out the words inside him, "I'm not a big man." Instead he laid a hand on the shoulder of the man who had shouted at him and asked him, "Can I help?"

At first the answer was the same sullen silence. One of the men swam out with two lengths of rope around his waist and came back after tying them to the overturned lorry. The land ends of the ropes were tied to the fender of the first lorry on the bank, and its driver started the motor. The lorry started backward, stopped, then moved again. But immediately one of the ropes snapped just a foot from the fender it was tied to.

"Wet them," Baako said. "Wet both ropes."

The driver who had shouted at him gave him a long look, his eyes shining dully in the dark, before going to untie the other rope, then dragging both to the water and immersing them. The driver in the lorry drove forward and the wet ropes were tied on again. The engine jumped to life; the lorry struggled a few moments, then made a break, going a few yards back and to the side. Over the water the movement created expanding ripples on the surface.

Two driver's mates jumped into the water, diving down when they got to the center of the widening circles. The fourth time up they swam heavily to the bank and the body was between them. They left it a little distance up on the bank, the lorry's headlights throwing a bare glint off the top of it.

Juana went to the body and bent to examine it.

"What does she want?" a voice asked.

"She's perhaps the doctor," another answered, a woman's.

"Oh."

Juana turned and called Baako. "Help me turn him. The water has to come out."

Baako held the body by its left shoulder. Two drivers joined them; one took the other shoulder and the other replaced Juana, taking the legs. The body when lifted caught the full light from the lorry; the head had been crushed so it was long and flat, and it hung limply till another man came to hold it up from the neck. Water dripped off the entire body, and when it was turned round and laid down a sudden stream gurgled out of the open mouth, trickling back down toward the river.

A tall woman, the one who had spoken, came close, took off her covercloth and covered the corpse with it; the soft rain made her naked back shine in the light. She was not weeping. Once she spoke again, but it was to herself, a small sound of regret:

"Aaah Skido."

Baako asked the driver closest to him, "His wife?"

"I don't know." The sound had anger in it and the driver turned hurriedly away. The others began to go off also, except for two men who first turned to Juana and Baako, said thanks, then took the corpse and went back up the road with it, disappearing in the night after the tall woman.

Going back to the rest house Baako wished he could walk faster. The coldness in his back was spreading down and inward into every bone in him, and he was sweating over all his body under the wetness of his clothes.

Once inside, he closed the shutters against the moist wind and after drying himself got into bed beside Juana. Her body was warm. He pressed himself against her, wanting her warmth against the chill in him. She had added a blanket to the top sheet and she pulled both over their heads. She took his head between her hands and he kissed her in the dark, feeling very weak. She rubbed his nipple gently, once, and it was pure pain but it made him hard, and she turned slightly and took him into herself, lying motionless in his embrace.

"Just stay in me, Baako," she said.

He moved deeper, searching her for more of her warmth, his head filling with a fear of nameless heavy things descending upon him, pushing him to seek comfort in her. He pulled her completely to himself. She was warm against him, but in a moment he became aware she too was shivering. They lay together, neither moving.

8 : Nsu

HE HAD SLEPT deeply. Waking up, knowing there'd be no more work to go to, he had to shed a strong desire to plunge back into the night's oblivion, and a deep-eating weakness pervaded his body. He got up and got dressed, wearing a *batakari* over a shirt. He went over to the bottom drawer, moved his notebooks aside and picked up the script sheets he'd brought home. He hadn't known there'd already been so much wasted work. He took the loose sheets first, then the finished scripts, and walked out.

In front of the kitchen he found Efua and Naana sitting by a coal pot fire just started.

"That is you, Baako," Naana said. "I give you the dawn."

"Morning," he said.

"Is there somethng I can do for you?" Efua said, smiling.

"Do you need the fire just now?" he asked.

"Not for a while. You want it?"

"I've got to burn some papers."

"Your work?" Efua squinted up into his face.

He nodded, then bent to pick up the coal pot. He was on his way down the kitchen stairs to the end yard when he felt his grandmother's touch on his arm.

"Why do you keep following him?" Efua shouted after them.

"I'm not following anybody," Naana said firmly, quietly. "I need to be near the fire."

She had brought her stool and sat a yard from the coal pot.

"Baako," she called in a whisper.

"Yes?"

"It was a lie," she said, and laughed softly. "I'm not really cold. I wanted to be with you."

"Is there anything?" he asked.

"Your asking itself shows the answer would be strange to you."

"Maybe it won't."

"I have such strong feelings here for you," Naana said, placing a hand just below her breast, "it's a good thing I was sent so far ahead of you. Had I come in your age, some nameless things might have happened in this family."

Baako laughed.

"Listen to him laugh. You think your grandmother is crazy this morning. You're also so young. You're among those who think a woman's lovegift dies with age. It doesn't die. It takes a strong spirit, though, to make it move again."

"You're talking to the wrong spirit, right now," he said. Taking the script that lay uppermost on the pile, he tore it up and placed the pieces on the fire. The papers curled, turned brown, then became a flame.

"Your mother asked if it was your work," Naana said, "you didn't answer."

"I said yes."

"Why then are you burning it?"

"To forget."

"It wasn't good work?"

"I don't know. It was never used."

He dropped the stapled sheets whole onto the coals and waited till they were consumed and their charred remains floated up, single bits suspended in the air, drifting downward into the dust of the yard.

When he came to the loose sheets of the unfinished treatments he found himself, against his own will, unable to let them go. The typed words held his eyes, bringing back to his mind images that had risen there and been caught, to be condemned to uselessness. He let a title page fall into the fire. It had a short caption on it:

THE ROOT.

As it burned the synopsis it had covered drew his eyes.

THROUGH REPETITIVE USE OF IMAGE AND SOUND
IMPRINT IDEA OF VIOLENCE, UNPLEASANT, STRONG, IRRESISTIBLE,
ATTACKING THE VIEWER, INVADING HIS EYES, ASSAULTING HIS
EARS.
MATCH SHARP SOUNDS WITH ABSTRACT IMAGES OF AGENTS OF
THIS VIOLENCE, ALL OF WHICH SHOULD BE LONG, SEVERELY

LINEAR, SHARP-EDGED PILLARS, SHAFTS, ALL WHITE
SUPERIMPOSED ON RECIPIENTS OF VIOLENCE,
VAGUE FLUID FORMS FILLING SCREEN,
CIRCULAR, YIELDING, SOFT, ALL BLACK.
TITLES
ACCOMPANIED BY QUIET BACKGROUND MUSIC WITH FREQUENT
DISSONANT LEAPING SOUNDS BREAKING IT UP
VIDEO: VIOLENT THRUSTS OF AGENTS INTO RECIPIENTS IN TIME
WITH THESE MUSICAL BREAKS.
THE RECIPIENTS IN THEIR VISCOUS NEAR-FLUIDITY
DISINTEGRATE UNDER THE IMPACT
THEN COME QUIVERING ROUND EACH IMPLANTED
AGENT.
BY THE END OF CREDITS WHEN CAMERA PULLS BACK FOR LS
SCREEN IS COVERED WITH A CIRCULAR, DARK EXPANSE, THE
RECIPIENT
THROUGH WHICH THE WHITE AGENTS STICK OUT AT REGULAR
INTERVALS, LOOKING LIKE ROWS OF SOLDIERS AT ATTENTION
BUT ALSO HAVING SOME OF THE AIR OF CROSSES IN A MILITARY
CEMETERY.
MUSIC DOWN
DISSOLVE TO
LS: OVERVIEW, COASTAL VILLAGE, QUIET, CIRCULAR, DARK.
NIGHT.
ON HILL IN DISTANCE, MASSIVE WHITE STRUCTURE OF SLAVE
CASTLE.
MS: SECTION OF CASTLE,
GUNS POINTING OVER VILLAGE,
PILE OF CANNON BALLS BESIDE THEM.
SENTRY PACING.
CUT TO VILLAGE.
HOUSE WITH ROUND WINDOW OPENING TO SMALL VIEW OF
CASTLE.
THREE WOMEN AND TWO MEN SITTING, STARING MUTE AT FLOOR.
CHILD LOOKING OUT THROUGH WINDOW.

At the production meeting when he'd presented this treatment,
Asante-Smith had stopped him just here and asked, "What is it
about?"

"Slavery."

"Why such a choice of topic?"

"How do you mean, why?"

"You understand me, Mr. Onipa," said Asante-Smith, with a small yawn. "Look, we're a free, independent people. We're engaged in a gigantic task of nation building. We have inherited a glorious culture, and that's what we're here to deal with."

"Slavery is a central part of that culture, isn't it?"

Around the table everyone was sitting very still and quiet.

"Do you have any others?" Asante-Smith asked suddenly.

"There's more of the first, *The Root*," Baako said.

"Do you have others?"

"I'd like to finish this."

"Look, don't waste time. I have an appointment at twelve."

"There's another here, *The Brand*," Baako said.

"What's that about?"

"Survival."

"Mr. Onipa," said Asante-Smith, "I know what the trouble is with you. You're too abstract in your approach to our work. For instance, what you've just said has nothing to do with our people's culture — all this slavery, survival, the brand."

"It has everything to do with it," Baako answered, surprised at the force of his own anger. Asante-Smith was looking casually at him. "You know of Doctor Aggrey."

"Yes, indeed. Grandfather of the nation," Asante-Smith said, leaning back and smiling. "Also the founder of my old school, Achimota. Yours, too, I hear, Mr. Onipa."

"I took the title from him. 'I am a brand plucked from the burning.'"

"Oh, did he say that?"

"Yes, he did," Baako said. "And meant every letter of it."

"Well," Asante-Smith said, with some uneasiness, "Aggrey was an honest man, an educator, a very great educator indeed."

"Good for him," Baako said. "As a matter of fact, he was talking about his own education. That's what the sentence was about."

"Hmm," said Asante-Smith. "I don't see what it has to do with the national culture and our work here."

"I thought it was obvious. The educated elite runs this place."

Asante-Smith said nothing, but his frown had turned into a happy smile, and he was nodding.

"So," Baako continued, "this Aggrey kind of attitude is

important. The educated really thinking of the people here as some kind of devils in a burning hell, and themselves the happy plucked ones, saved."

"Just read what you have down, Mr. Onipa."

This one had consumed more of him in its conception, and he had hoped to make something good and complete out of it; his hand moved heavily now he was burning it, hesitating over the pages.

SINGLE DARK CIRCLE FILLING SCREEN, REPRESENTING THE WEAK PERIPHERY, LARGE ENVIRONMENT, HABITAT OF THE OPPRESSED.
ON WHICH A SQUARE IS SUPERIMPOSED, WHITE, THE TOUGH CONCRETIZED FORTIFICATION.
PAN TO
SIDE ELEVATION, SAME.
LS: LADDER LEADING FROM WEAK CIRCLE TO STRONG SQUARE.
CU: THE LADDER IS MADE UP OF THE SHOULDERS OF INHABITANTS OF THE LOWER LEVEL, THE OPPRESSED.
MS: HERO, WHOSE FACE CAMERA NEVER SHOWS IN CU, IS SEEN MAKING THE CLIMB. AT EACH STEP HE HAS TO
JUSTIFY HIS CLIMB, TO HIMSELF, AND TO THE
SHOULDERS UNDER HIM.
BALANCE GETS PRECARIOUS NEAR THE SQUARE.
JUSTIFICATION CONSISTS OF HERO'S REITERATED PROMISE HE'S ONLY CLIMBING UP TO FIND THE MEANS TO LIBERATE THOSE WHOSE SHOULDERS
HE'S CLIMBED ON. THIS THEME ESTABLISHED IN AN
ENTHUSIASM RALLY
WHOSE PURPOSE IS TO DRUM UP MATERIAL AND MORAL SUPPORT FOR THE HERO'S CLIMBING EFFORT.
AT END HERO HAS ARRIVED AND IS CLINGING
DANGEROUSLY TO THE SHEER SIDE OF THE SQUARE.
NOT GOING BACK DOWN. IT'S PLAIN
THE CLIMB ITSELF, THE PROCESS OF GETTING TO THE SQUARE, HAS INJECTED INTO HIS BEING AN ADDICTION TO WAYS AND HABITS DIAMETRICALLY OPPOSED TO THE LIBERATOR'S CAREER.
OTHER CHARACTERS:
1. OLD MAN. A COMPLETE CYNIC, LIVES FLAT ON HIS BACK AS A MATTER OF PRINCIPLE, EXPLAINING HE WANTS TO MAKE SURE NO

ONE USES HIS SHOULDERS AS A LADDER.

AT ENTHUSIASM RALLY, FOR INSTANCE, HE ARGUES WITH THE INFINITE PATIENCE OF CERTAIN TRUTH (FROM HIS NORMAL POSITION ON THE GROUND) THAT THE HOT PROMISES ARE WORTH NOTHING, THAT THE HERO AS HE RISES WILL GET ACCUSTOMED TO BREATHING THE AIR UP THERE AND WANT TO STAY, NOT TO RETURN TO THE MUD. HE SAYS HE DOESN'T MIND ANYONE GETTING UP THERE, BUT AS FOR KILLING HIMSELF TO GET THEM UP THERE, NO THANKS.

2. MIDDLE-AGED MAN, NICKNAMED "OUR PROGRESS."

HOPEFUL PROLIX SOUL WHO SEES THE SALVATION OF THE CIRCLE AS A MATTER OF INCREASING NUMBERS OF INHABITANTS CLIMBING

UP AND AWAY INTO THE SQUARE. HEAVEN FOR HIM WOULD BE THE FINAL DEATH OF THE CIRCLE AND THE EXPANSION OF THE SQUARE THROUGH ABSORBING WHAT WAS INSIDE THE CIRCLE.

3. WEEPING WOMAN. IGNORED BY EVERYBODY, BUT PERENNIALLY WRINGING HER HANDS AND SAYING SHE'S OLD ENOUGH TO KNOW THE SQUARE IS THERE NOT TO ABSORB THE CIRCLE BUT TO WIPE IT OUT. OCCASIONALLY SHE SPEAKS AS IF THE CIRCLE'S

INHABITANTS WERE INDEED DEAD ALREADY, CALLING THEM GHOSTS, SPOOKS, NSAMANFO, ZOMBIES, ETC.

4. ANGRY WOMAN, CAUGHT UP IN A LONG SLEEP OF DESPAIR FROM WHICH SHE WAKES OCCASIONALLY TO CHANT DREAMS OF DESTRUCTION

AGAINST THE SQUARE.

5. THE THINKER. AN INTELLECTUAL, REBELLIOUS WITHIN HIS INTELLECTUAL'S IMPOTENCE. CONSTANTLY AND VISIBLY THINKING,

HE IS NORMALLY IN A STATE CLOSE TO CATATONIA, EXCEPT WHEN SOME LIBERATING INSIGHT GIVES HIM FLASHES OF MANIC ELOQUENCE WITH WHICH TO PREACH HIS FAVORITE THEME:

TO DEFEAT THE SQUARE WITH THE FORCE OF THE SQUARE ITSELF. TWO CHORUSES:

1. THE INHABITANTS OF THE CIRCLE, A CHORUS OF QUIET, DENSE DEFEAT,

AND 2. ABOVE THEM THE SQUARE PEOPLE IN WHITE-WHITE LIKE PERENNIAL COLONIAL SCHOOLBOYS, HARD WITH AN EXTERIOR SHINE,

EXHIBITIONISTIC, SELF-GRATULATING.

SOME OF THESE ROAM THE CIRCLE IN COMPACT CORPS, SELECTING AT INTERVALS PROSPECTIVE CLIMBERS, ISOLATING THEM WITH A REPEATED RITUAL OF CONGRATULATION AND SUSTAINED PRAISE.

A loud cough had stopped him this time too, in the Production Conference Room.

"You have some very peculiar concerns," Asante-Smith said.

"Peculiar to whom?" he asked. But again only the silence answered him. Looking at the other faces he found not a trace of interest, nor even, it seemed to him, of life. Everything stayed suspended. Slowly he took his notebook in his left hand, balanced it open for a while, then snapped it shut.

"At any rate," said Asante-Smith, "we have no film or tape for drama."

From the far end of the table a different voice spoke. "Some new tape just came in, sir."

"I know," Asante-Smith answered. "It's all booked. There are important national holidays ahead. Founder's Day, Liberation Day, the Freedom Festival of Youth. And Independence Day itself isn't very far off. We'll be busy."

"Taking pictures of the Head of State?" Baako had not intended it as a question, but his words and tone seemed to have turned everyone to stone, and Asante-Smith was staring open-mouthed at him.

"Yes, Mr. Onipa," Asante-Smith said finally, "we'll be taking pictures of your elders who freed this nation."

Gariba, Aryeetey, Samoah, Crabbe, Easilfie, Baiden, Ashong, Van der Puije, Mensah, Kofie: cameramen, producers, another writer, silent, impassive. Baako's eyes came back to Asante-Smith, and he heard the cold voice.

"Does anyone else have anything to say?"

Still the silence.

"Good, we'll cut this short. I have to go," Asante-Smith said. Then, "By the way, the sets are being distributed today. The highest officials from the Residence are the Presidential Secretariat will get theirs first, then the Ministries. Senior Officers here at Ghanavision will get what's left."

"I thought . . ." Baako began, then decided not to continue. But Asante-Smith was looking at him, a deliberate, waiting expression on his face.

"Yes, Mr. Baako, you thought?"

"What about the scheme to put the sets all over the country, in the villages?"

"Yes," Asante-Smith said, "what about it?" Then with a small chuckle he rose from the table and walked out, calling for his driver. Everyone relaxed, but nothing was said concerning the meeting. Judging by the faces now suddenly alive once more, it hadn't happened.

Baako went out of the conference room, descended the stairs and at the main lobby turned left, heading along the corridor cutting the production building into its two huge studios. As he came out into the sun he saw the big gates to the left studio had been thrown wide open. The studio itself was filled with sets in brown cartons painted over with the bright silver colors of a brand sign: a torch with an electric bolt shooting out of it in place of an ordinary flame, above the Japanese and English lettering. There were lines of cars and official vans waiting out in the driveway, into which several barebacked men were busy piling sets. Off the curb another man stood, a pencil stuck in his hair, taking a small chit for each driver as he came up and shouting a curt order to the porters, occasionally exchanging words with some driver.

"Three sets."

"Three."

"Five."

"Five."

"One."

"One."

"Twelve . . . Hey, wait a mo. What the hell you mean, twelve?"

"I be Police Inspector-Genal Kraka him driver. If him say twelve, e be twelve. Paper no lie, no be so?"

"All right, twelve."

"Four for Colonel Blay."

"Four."

"Two."

"Two."

The cars drew off after each loading, making a slow line like a funeral cortege, carrying their television sets. Baako watched them, their hypnotic movement absorbing him for a long time, till the last car went off too and he was suddenly wondering what would happen next. A weariness filled his body, so that he remained leaning against the huge wall, just watching what was happening in the sun. As if someone had summoned them all at once a crowd of Senior Officers descended into the studio, dragging out sets and inspecting them in the light outside, then walking off to their cars with the ones they'd picked. Gariba ran by, selected a set, then on his way to the car park stopped beside Baako.

"Look, man, it's no use standing there worrying," he said panting. "Go in and get yours. You'll want one anyway." He chuckled and tried to smile, but what Baako saw on his face was the usual ambiguous expression, midway from cynicism to shame. Gariba raised his eyebrows, giggled and lurched off with his set.

There was only one left. One of the Senior Officers had looked at it, found it unpleasing to his eye and rejected it. It stood there beside its carton, and the air just above it was beginning to shake a little with the heat. Baako saw two men walking toward the studios from the Technicians' prefab down the road. They were talking to each other, and laughing; but suddenly it seemed the same single thought had come into both of them and possessed them — they began running forward, very fast. The smaller man was easily the faster, and he got to the last television set some yards ahead of his friend. But this second man was of a heavier build, and as he too came to the set he did not check his speed but bent slightly and ran with deliberate force into the smaller one. The first man was knocked off balance, though he did not fall, not immediately, for the open gate took him on its edge and crushed him body and head between itself and the heavy friend. For some moments the small man seemed entirely bewildered at what was happening. He looked around him with a very happy grin on his face, and Baako thought he was about to laugh. But then a weak sound escaped his lips, a feeble moan of pain, and a first, glossy drip of blood slipped down the left side of his shirt front, stopping just above the top of the pocket, as he slid in a queerly relaxed motion down to the ground, staring at his friend in a quiet, peaceful astonishment.

The strong one laughed a laugh with no regret in it, looking at his fallen companion, then stopped and took the set in his glad embrace, his eyes still on the other. He, the weak one, had the air of one who had given up any notion of continuing the painful contention, but as the strong man hefted the set with his muscular arms and strode confidently forward with it, the fallen man groped and reached a stone sharing the ground with him, and in an unexpected movement hurled it with a hard, desperate force.

The new set had only a last, brief moment in which to reflect the sunlight in the pearly smoothness of its screen, and then where the brittle glass had been, the hunk of concrete smashed in and left a hole through which it crashed against the copper circuitry within.

The victor also stood a petrified moment, then dropped the destroyed set, letting out a groan that must have risen all the way from the wreckage of his hot inner desire. He took one quick, desolate look at his shattered dream and then he leaped after his triumphant victim. But the little man, howling his fear in unashamed relief, was running again, putting a wider distance between his friend and himself, weaving gracefully sideways off the road to let the Director's incoming car pass.

Asante-Smith stepped out and waved the driver on to the car park, then he drew near, saw the wreck of the last set and looked up from it into Baako's face.

"What happened?" Asante-Smith asked.

"I don't really know," Baako answered him, shaking his head.

"Who caused this mess?"

"Funny, that's the question I've been asking myself," Baako said, keeping his voice very calm.

Asante-Smith squinted suspiciously into Baako's face, then turned his attention to a passing laborer.

"Hey you! Come. Clear this mess!"

"Yessah sah!"

Asante-Smith went up to his office but in Baako's mind there was an indelible close-up of the Director's smile when, at some other production meeting, Baako had explained his desire to find out more about the illiterate people's images and myths for use in his work.

The idiot had been right to smile, though. Baako felt a growing lightness going down all the way to his heels. At the same time he was driven by a compelling urge to walk out, past the control gate, left at the roundabout, straight past the Military Hospital, then right after that up Cantonments Road, trying to break the disturbing seam of thought with walking. When he reached Juana's bungalow he lay back on the veranda, closed his eyes against the sun's slanting rays, and waited.

"*Qué pasó?*"

"Nothing, Juana." He went in with her and waited while she mixed drinks for herself and him.

He took a sip and asked her, "May I use your machine?"

"Christ!" she said. "What makes you so formal?"

She brought the typewriter and a box of paper, and he tried to type the letter he'd thought of but gave up after a while.

"Fucking Spanish keyboard!" he muttered.

"Hey, man, not everybody had the great good fortune to be colonized by the Anglo-Saxons. Here, I'll do it for you if it isn't a ten-volume history of the Great Imperial Heritage."

"It isn't too long," he said.

"O.K." She took the typewriter and changed the paper. "Shoot."

"Seven stroke three Asafo Street," he began, "Kaneshie, Accra. Date. Dear Personnel Officer, comma, line. I quit."

"Oh no, Baako," Juana laughed, "they'll think you're crazy."

"Let them. Paragraph. I'm giving the required month's notice, starting from today. Line. Sincerely. Line. Baako Onipa."

"My god," Juana said, "What happened, man?"

*

The flames vanished over the last pages, leaving the bowl of the coal pot covered with fragile, charred remnants, red where the fire was still not dead, white near the middle with ash.

"Why are you so quiet?" Naana asked.

"It's finished," he said.

"You didn't tell me what it was."

"I was trying to say things in my mind, to let other people see."

"That sounds like a priest."

He laughed weakly, and rose to go.

"Don't go," Naana said. "Sit with me. You're sad, aren't you? I can't understand why you always refuse to tell me what is happening."

He sat by her, and saw the strain in her face disappear.

"Will you talk to me? Not now, if you don't want to, but another day?"

"I will, Naana, but not today."

9 : Dam

A STEADY FEELING reached him from the face above his, looking down. But open or closed his eyes hurt, his head, his whole body hurt, his eyes were not steady and he could not tell what the look meant — concern, fear, love, resentment, hate: he found no way to get away from the mixed uncertainty. He closed his eyes again to escape the face. What he wanted was not any concerned face, least of all the worried motherface staring down dark against the bulb he wanted to turn off. He wanted sleep for a body bruised all over from the fever within, though he was tired of lying helpless so many hours, three days already in bed, too ill and too weak to get up when he wanted to. He turned on his belly to lessen his discomfort. That hurt too, and the sheet under him felt wet and clammy from his sweat.

His mother was wiping sweat off his neck and shoulders with her cloth. Her movements were gentle, but his body felt raw and he had to hold himself in to keep from telling her to stop, and he was aware that he had begun again to shiver, slightly.

"You're very ill, Baako," his mother said, as if she had only just come to realize it.

"I am, yes. But what a funny thing to say now."

"You need help."

"I need to rest. I'll be all right."

"You said that when it began. But you didn't rest, and now you're worse."

"I couldn't rest," he said, wishing he could go to sleep immediately and not have to keep talking anymore.

"I know," his mother said. "I could hear you, all those nights."

"Not so many."

"Even one single night is a long time when you're needing rest.

But all you did was type, all these nights."

"I kept you awake, didn't I?" he asked uncertainly.

"No," his mother answered, "it wasn't the sound of your machine. I couldn't sleep myself. I have my own troubles, and they keep me up. Your door is closed, and mine. The noise is very little; I have to listen to hear it, far away. It makes me think of termites hidden in wood, talking."

"Termites talking. Why talking?" He almost laughed.

"The noise you make is small like that, going on all the time. It isn't that I chose to think of termites, but that is what I thought of." Her explanation sounded funny to him, and he opened his mouth to prevent his laughter from being tense and painful; the sound he made was like a wide open sigh.

"You feel better now," his mother said, "trying to laugh at me." He nodded.

"Yes," she continued, "the sweat isn't coming anymore. But still your eyes . . ." Baako turned his eyes away from her, closing them. His neck hurt more than the rest of his body; he wanted to close his ears, but he heard her saying, "You look so tired. What is it you can't stop writing?"

"Just things I've thought about," he said.

"You should try not to think. Not too much."

"What do you mean?"

"You know," she said. "You don't eat well when you start that typing. I've watched you. And then you don't sleep."

A fractured thought crossed his mind. The urge to trap it before it disappeared made him forget the general pain of his body. He reached down to the floor to take up his notebook; a pen marked the last page he had come to, and taking it he began to write:

RE CARGO CULTS: They seem to make a certain kind of clear sense, here too. So how far, how close are we to Melanesia? It can be seen as a pure, rockbottom kind of realism, the approach that accepts what happens at this moment in this place and raises it to the level of principle. A reality principle par excellence, this. Two distinct worlds, one here, one out there, one known, the other unknown except in legend and dream. But the twilight area between the two is also an area of knowledge, twisted knowledge perhaps, but knowledge resulting from real information in the form of incoming goods, outgoing people. The main export to the other world is people. The true dead going back to the ancestors, the ritual dead (all that libation and talk like a funeral when I was going on the plane — it happens for almost everyone who goes. I wonder if the ritual is still understood. Ask Naana later, try to find out what she sees and knows of this). At any rate it is clearly understood that the been-to has chosen, been awarded, a certain kind of death. A beneficial death, since cargo follows his return. Not just cargo, but also importance, power, a radiating influence capable of touching ergo elevating all those who in the first instance have suffered the special bereavement caused by the been-to's going away. Jesus, how neatly the most natural impulsive reactions (tears, fear, hope, pride, joy) find a place in this stultifying pattern. So very natural. In a way, there is nothing all that special about the been-to's coming, given the logic of the cargo system itself. After all, in the unelaborated system — where the been-to has yet to make his appearance, and there is no intermediary between the earth below and the sky above, no visible flesh and blood intermediary at any rate — the human being once dead is in his burial considered as having been exported to the other world. A return is expected from his presence there: he will intercede on behalf of those not yet dead, asking for them what they need most urgently: rain perhaps if their crops are dry, an end to rain if there has been a punishing surfeit. Needs dictated by instant survival and subsistence requirements. Plus prestige for those closest, the immediate bereaved. Hand go hand come. The been-to here then only fleshes out the pattern. He is the ghost in person returned to live among men, a powerful ghost understood to the extent that he behaves like a powerful ghost, cargo and all. Meets established, well-known expectations handsomely, *functions* like a ghost (look into Afro-American usage of word spook, also West Indian myth-clusters around the zombie idea), accepts the ghost role and feels perfectly at home in it. In many ways the been-to cum ghost is and has to be a transmission belt for cargo. Not a maker, but an intermediary. Making takes too long, the intermediary brings quick gains. The gaining circle is narrower, it is true, but with rockbottom realism inherent in the system the close ones find nothing strange in it. It is life. The idea the ghost could be a maker, apart from being too slow-breaking to interest those intent on living as well as the system makes possible, could also have something of excessive pride in it. Maker, artist, but also maker, god. It is presumably a great enough thing for a man to rise to be an intermediary between other men and the gods. To think of being a maker oneself could be sheer unforgiveable sin. The witches? *Ntan*. Pride here. Hubris for the Greeks. Did the

Melanesians think of this? Must go to Legon, see if there is anything useful in the Library there. The most impressive thing in the system is the wall-like acceptance of the division. Division of labor, power, worlds, everything. Not inherent in the scheme, this acceptance. Inherent mainly in the INTERPRETATION people give the system. Saves thought, I suppose.

While he was writing the fever rose in him again, and he could feel the sweat oozing out of him, hot and then immediately chilling. The wetness went all the way down to his sole, and his toes when he moved them were slippery against each other. But he could not stop writing till he had caught the fugitive thought and put it down, and then he relaxed thankfully on the bed, surprised to hear himself breathing as if he had been holding in his breath too long. His mother had not left.

"Where is Melanesia?"

He had not thought of her reading what he had written, and now he wished she would go away after this one question. "Islands in the Pacific," he said.

"And cargo cults, what are those?" Into her voice a quality had come that he hated in a way he himself could still not fully understand. When his mother spoke like that, diminishing her voice to make it sound childish and unknowing, he did not have to see the usual accompanying smile to feel disgust. It was partly, he supposed, because the voice and the look were always so stupidly untrue; but he was tired and did not want to think his feelings out. He turned to look at his mother.

"I have to be alone now."

"I know," she answered. "I'll go in a moment. But what is it really, what you wrote?"

"Something that occurred to me, a thought, that's all," he said.

"For whom?"

"Myself."

"You wrote it to yourself," she said slowly, her voice musing. Thinking he had made himself plain enough he added nothing to help her. "But that is a little like having a conversation with no one, talking alone to yourself."

"Well, if you want . . ." he said.

"Baako," she asked, "is that the way it was before you came, when you were ill?"

"Is that what?"

"Did you write things to yourself?"

For moments he did not find words for an answer; he just thought of the words, heard the concern with which his mother had spoken them, but heard something else too that made him forget the pain in his body in the anger of the moment.

"Efua, I want to sleep," he said.

His mother went out in haste, silently, leaving the light on. He had got up naked to turn it off when in one long moment too many things started happening all at once inside his body. His mouth filled up as if his saliva were flowing to escape some pressure from below, and it would never stop. His eyes felt out of the sockets, floating detached in a steady blast of warm air getting hotter every moment. There was one sharp needlepoint of pain boring into his skull from the top of his head, and the cold line along his neck was spreading. There was no more room in his mouth, and the moisture was in his throat, threatening to choke him. He ran, forgetting every pain and weakness, straight to the bathroom and had just enough strength to kneel with his head hanging over the edge of the tub before the huge vomiting fever came draining out of him, tearing itself out of a body too weak to help or resist it, dropping in waves that left him shivering, tasting all through his head the thick bitterness of his own closed-up bile. Then he felt his head go hot without any warning, so he let it hang under the tap and turned the water on, bathing his head and neck, washing the vomit down the drain. His whole body felt warm too; he ran the shower and washed himself quickly under it, then thoroughly soaked and comforted he hurried back to his room, looking for a towel. On the way in he saw his mother standing at her door; he smiled at her, winked and said, "I'm all right, Efua." She smiled back at him, but the astonishment he had noticed on her face did not disappear.

Once in his room he took a towel from the top drawer of his chest and dried himself. The walk on the bare cement floor had started him feeling cold again, and when he felt dry enough he drew his body into a tight ball on the bed, covering himself completely with his cloth and the top blanket, oblivious of the light. He would gladly have gone to sleep, but that sweet slide was once more interrupted by the continuing trail of the idea he had been writing about, and he had to write again. Reaching for the notebook he heard the gate make a noise and thought cursorily that at this time of night it must be the wind shaking it, so he dismissed the sound and turned his mind to his writing.

CARGO MENTALITY. The expectancy, the waiting for bounty dropping from the sky through benign intercession of dead ancestors, the beneficent ghosts. Out there in ancestral territory beyond the cemetery the goods are available in abundance, no doubt at all about that in Melanesian cargo mythology. Lleweni Ruve: what a beautiful name for sheer illusion, though. Wish I had taken notes, or had the books somewhere within reach now. The waiting not a simple expectation, but something more active. An integral part of the waiting is an active expression of strong belief that the cargo will come, i.e., the phenomenon of hope is incomplete without an incorporated act of faith. In Melanesia the burning of food crops, the slaughtering of indispensable livestock, all those pigs destroyed: an earnest of mortal faith, of the belief men have that it is unthinkable the ghosts should fail — if the ritual games are played with sufficient seriousness. First I had thought this rather extreme, and assumed it would be far-fetched to look for an analogy here with cargo expectancy behavior in mind. But then two, three? already . . . months ago I was knocked flat hearing that Production Assistant talk about the things he believed. Poor guy, I do not remember his name, but why can't I? He couldn't have known what a lot of meaning his straight expression of his faith had for me. Said he was a practicing nexologist. I was curious and asked him what was that, and he was very happy to explain, speaking not only to me, perhaps he looks for converts wherever he can. I confess it was a thrill to hear him define nexus so well, everything in the world connected, the air itself some connecting fluid, each man a connecting center node set in the nexus. The fact of connection meaning consequence: here I wondered if he understood what he was implying or was sloganizing with doctrines swallowed, but I would not have interrupted him for all the world, though I was definite, looking at their faces, that the others were no longer with him, though they would have liked to be. The example he gave of the behavior of a practicing nexologist I thought was cute, and then its connection with cargo expectancy, that bowled me over when I got to it. Summarizing: the nexologist prays through action. Example: a nexologist wakes up one morning, counts his wealth and finds he's broke, only pennies between him and the world. Like me, he says smiling. The practicing nexologist under such conditions does not despair, throw up his arms, lose faith in himself. On the contrary: the hopeless-looking moment is the moment not only for hope, but for the expression of faith in hope. I had to unravel that a bit, but within his system it made sense thus far. So what would the nexologist, practicing, do? Man smiled at me. Why, he would take his last coins, find his way to a crossways, then scatter the last of his wealth in all directions. Now that wealth would be bound to return to the scatterer in one form or another, multiplied like grain seed. He was reciting doctrine again, straight. I asked him why, deliberately refusing to accept the natural grain analogy for human coins. So he said the scattering would be answered by a wished-for return because of the nexus, because the nexus meant connections, and no such act of prayer ever took place unconnected to results that could look like magic to the blind. But there was one important proviso: sincerity. The scatterer, he said, doctrinal again, must believe heart and soul in the scattering, otherwise he was struggling against connections in the nexus, which would be like working against himself. Ended with a triumphant "Try it!" to me. So without deliberately asking for it I had got in a clear raw state a metamorphosis of the cargo myth here. Kill the pigs, burn the crop and wait with faith. Throw the last coins, brokeman. So how close are we to the Melanesian islands? How close is everybody?

The softness of the tail end of his thoughts displeased him, but he felt too tired to argue with what he had written. Later, certainly, he would go back to it and see. He knew he wouldn't have the strength now to rise and switch off the light; he did not seem able even to take his eyes off the bulb, and the luminous circle burned a sound into his head, a sound like a power engine not too far away pulsing up and down each second, charging the air with an eternal rising, falling smoothness. The night outside was deep.

He heard a car coming up the street. He had expected it to pass, but its noise stopped at the wall and a short time after that car doors shut in the night and the gate into the yard opened with a loud noise. This time there was no mistaking it for the work of the wind. There were voices in the yard: first a man's deep voice, a sound he could not remember too clearly hearing in the yard; then a woman spoke, his mother Efua, followed by a questioning male voice that was clearly Kwesi's. The voices fell quiet and were replaced by footfalls on the porch. The hall door made a noise like a surly complaint when they came in, and then there was an undecided knock on his door. He asked who it was, and only his mother answered, but all three who had come in from outside entered. He had been reading the last line in his notebook over and over again, and it was some moments after the three had walked into his room that he took his eyes off the page and looked up into the faces above him. Staring at them he wondered immediately why they should look so plainly mournful, like bearers of some bad news he knew already, news they had no stomach for talking about but which would have to come out between them one way or another. In the faces he sensed an assumption of some terrible knowledge shared, and in spite of himself he wondered what it could really be.

Since there was no one there willing to speak first he asked them, "Is anything the matter?"

The third face was a face he did not remember seeing in a long time. Now his uncle Foli bent over him to bring his face closer before he talked. It was a big face given a thicker, not a frailer look by the lines crossing it, holding in its heaviness eyes sunken so deep they seemed to float in identical little pools of very thin, yellowed blood.

"Oh no, nothing, Baako, don't be afraid, nothing," his uncle said, his face giving off so much fear Baako wondered what his question could have meant to him.

"But why are you here now?" he asked.

"You're ill, Baako," his mother answered.

He nodded. "I'll be all right, though, tomorrow."

"We'll get help for you, Baako, don't worry." His uncle was speaking again, near to choking with sorrow. "We'll take you where someone will take good care of you."

That final phrase stuck in his mind, took it along on quick swings between fear and love that seemed to breathe in conspiracy with the fever inside him. Take care of him, take good care of him, just take care of him, good care, care, take care of him! The three by his bedside disappeared, pushed out by a memory taken over by the mystery of a melody whose words had a twist that had troubled him before, more than once. A single female voice, clear and high against nothing, singing about desired ones telling you wicked, loving lies. Take care of you . . .

Thinking for some reason that it was very urgent not to lose sight of all the questions flowing from the cargo myth, he asked, "Where's Naana?" Immediately he wished he had not talked.

"Naana?" his mother asked. Her voice had dropped very low.

"I don't need to go anywhere," he said. "I'll be feeling fine."

"We're going with you," his uncle said.

"Yes, we'll go with you," Kwesi also said.

The sharp pain pricked inward from his skull again, and his throat heaved, bringing the taste of bile up into his mouth. He could not remember when last he had eaten meat, but the overcooked aftertaste of digested meat was on his tongue. He felt weak, and he knew he needed air. He tried then to rise, thinking of the window, but he collapsed softly back into the bed. He looked up and saw the serious faces returning his gaze, even grimmer now. He was glad they were there; he wished they would help him, he felt so weak.

"I am really sick," he said, half in astonishment.

"We'll go with you," someone said.

While getting dressed he felt he would never get through doing it with so little force left in him. He had to be helped on the way out, and he apologized several times for this, strangely getting no answer from his mother or the two men with her. In the car too he felt nauseous and far too weak to sit up straight, but when the car moved the wind rushing in revived him, and after a while he sat up and asked, "Where are we going?" But the only answer came from his mother, who said simply, "Don't worry, Baako. Rest."

He lay back in the seat and closed his eyes. The sound of the motor took in his mind the form of a lopsided wheel turning, each revolution a noise commanding: rest, rest, rest, rest, rest. But imperceptibly the message deepened and turned into something harrowing, going: rest, rest, rest in peace, rest, rest, rest in peace . . . The former sounds came back, and with them the lyrics about wicked loving lies, but now he was too tired to do anything but look out at the vanishing road and ask again, hoping he made a gentle, unfrightened sound this time, "But where are we going?" The only answer was that Kwesi and his mother, sitting on either side of him, each put a hand gently on his thigh. He noticed now he was in a protected position between his mother and Kwesi, leaving his uncle Foli alone in the front seat, driving. At the big circle the car turned halfway round and up the gentle rise to Boundary Road. The YWCA showed quickly gray and white against the night, then the unlit form of the Archives building on the right as the car reached the Asylum roundabout. No longer feeling the sickness in himself, aware only of one huge desire to break free of the familial hands restraining him, to get out into the air outside, Baako lunged brutally sideways across Kwesi's lap, grabbed the left door handle and opened the door, then he let it swing open, at the same moment shouting with all the force he could still gather, "Stop!"

The car screeched to a stop far from the curb, and profiting from the brief confusion within Baako shoved his way past Kwesi and out on the road. The three inside the car recovered and came out after him, the two men closing in.

"Leave me alone," he said. The men checked their forward movement and he asked them, "What are you doing to me? Where were we going?" But neither man answered; as if by prior agreement they moved again toward him. He saw his mother. In the darkness around, with the only light coming from the harsh concentrated beams at the circle, her eyes were visible, staring in fear — whether for him or of him he could not think. From her also there was no answer. Nothing but the two men advancing inexorably as he retreated, talking to them, asking unanswered questions, telling them to leave him alone. Then when he had almost relaxed and had grown intent on getting his pursuers to speak to him, Kwesi lunged out swiftly, unexpectedly, caught hold of his right arm and tried to force him down close to himself. His uncle Foli shook off his surprise and began in his turn to move cumbersomely in. Baako had only a moment of uncertainty, then choking at the thought of the capturing embrace he swung in desperation with his free left arm and the fist hit Kwesi's face hard, making him give out a pained gasp that brought no regret into Baako's mind, only a sour knowledge that he'd be lost now if he found no way to remain uncaught. The two were moving forward again, slowly. He ran.

The first minutes were difficult, but soon enough he began to feel a great freedom in movement. He ran back down the road, taking easy strides, keeping ahead of the panting pursuit, going back the way the car had come till he reached the Boundary Road junction, where he turned left instead of right, then coasted up the road till he could hear the two behind him no more. He turned to look, and saw them walking away. He relaxed. There was a lightness in him that made him think he was seeing himself from some point outside, looking down and seeing the last half hour all over again. Houses and low walls passed, then the night sign of the Avenida Hotel.

He was uneasy at the thought that this was also a return to a kind of beginning. Then, making up his mind to kill the uneasiness, he stopped running and walked deliberately down the remembered path of his first day back home. There was nothing around. He saw nothing in the alleyways there, except once suddenly the night eyes of a cat, a sight that forced him to lift his hands protectively to his own eyes, shuddering an involuntary shudder at the thought — where did it come from? — of bared claws leaping into naked eyes. All around there was only a silence that seemed endless. In the hotel annex there was no light on at any late traveler's window. Only one thing broke the silence once, very briefly: it was the wild unfriendly noise of invisible cats making love. A left turn in between close walls led to a narrow street. He walked down it, found a network of other narrow alleyways and streets to drift down in the Adabraka night, turned away when he saw knots of people in the distance still gathered around dancing oil flames, and reached the Ring Road feeling glad he was out now when the dual way looked so eternally peaceful. Two police jeeps came up the road from behind him, and as he crossed there was a single wood truck going the opposite way. Otherwise there was nothing on the road beside him.

He broke again into a run, the happy feeling rising in him that now he could run miles and miles and sense no tiredness. He clenched his fists and then let them go, feeling the fingers move individually; he moved his toes against each other in his sandals, and sweet relief flowed from the shifting of muscles seldom felt. He took a flying leap to avoid the rails at the level crossing, jumping twice, kept running all the way past the Guinea Press to the cemetery and right till the new roundabout, where he stopped and walked easily up the small rise along Link Road. Now he could feel pain. The sweat from his running brought with it a small tinge of the fever, and fear made him think of turning back. Even now he knew he could run all the way across Accra. Only when he thought of places he would be running to there was only one, and Juana, who lived in that one place, should still be away in her own country. He wished there were not so much loneliness around; that Juana had not had another country to go to when she needed rest. But her leave would be over in a matter of weeks at the worst, and she had even said she could be back long before then.

The pain in his head was on again, a vanishing white spark. He should take an aspirin, something, when he got back in. Coming down the last street he saw two cars now outside the gate, but it was a thing he could not care about now. The sickness was making him shake. When he entered he found his room empty. He locked the door and got into bed.

Out of nowhere a question came to worry him: how much money did he have in his wallet? He tried to forget it, couldn't, and got up to take the wallet from a trouser pocket. He shook it out and saw a couple of cedis fall on the bed, plus bus and cinema ticket stubs and a smooth oblong card. He switched off the light and tried to sleep. There was a pulse in his temple that would not let him sleep. Its beat carried words along, words that said this is nothing serious, nothing really, nothing, nothing, nothing; a foolish happening, gone tomorrow, really nothing, nothing, nothing. Then the throbbing wasted its insistence, seemed to stop entirely, leaving no sound, only a cold light spreading over endless ash deserts in the brain. No sound, no words, but there was a meaning all the same in the pitiless, timeless, implacable light: you know it is something, something dreadful has happened tonight, something worse is happening in you now, outside, everywhere, and you can escape, of course you can't, where would you go? Something happened, it wasn't nothing, not nothing: something awful, something, something. Stop thinking then and rest in peace, in peace, ha! don't stop thinking, don't drop into sleep, that would be the beginning of something, something something.

But the light in his head was too ashen, and dark brown circles fell welcomely over it, expanded out and away, yet reached inward first of all to include him so there were no more dangerous thoughts disturbing him, no nothings and no unknown something. All that inward space was taken by the rough texture of circles spinning into smoothness, moving away, turning in their outward movement, and a soft new humming sound, steady as the light but also comforting, warm, easy, not in any way fearful or disturbing. Before he slept he felt a hard edge against his side. The object when he held it up was a flat card with a luminous face. He read the middle line, the boldest — the rest remained a blur.

HENRY ROBERT HUDSON BREMPONG, BSC.

He threw the card on the floor. It slid along, stopping at the wall, its shiny face up, all the letters blurred in a green glow.

*

Panic woke him in the morning but soothing, peaceful subsidence followed immediately. He sensed the uncertainty not only within himself but also outside, in the house. If he could remember not to do anything to alarm anyone, things would be all right. He would go calmly to the bathroom, wash, come back like on any other day. The important thing was not to throw fear into anyone. He was beginning to feel very well, but then the cold half of the fever set in again. He lay in bed, waiting till the fever swung high into an unbearable hot flush, then he rose.

The bathroom door was closed. He returned to his room and waited long enough for two people to use the shower. The gate creaked and he looked out to see his mother going out to work. He wondered who exactly the two who had been in the bathroom could be. When he could hear no noises anymore he went in and took his shower.

He saw his notebook when he got back, and while getting dressed he opened it and looked again at the words of the previous night. He could not make them flow together; they remained separate words, separate letters. Something else was in his mind now. He was beginning again to feel too weak to follow the thought, so he wrote it also down. He would think of it later, perhaps, when he felt better.

Juana said she could be back before the end of the second month of her leave. She could be back already then. Bare possibility. May be nothing. Or again, something. Must find out. Later.

A chill starting in the side of his head made him shiver slightly, then passed. Thinking of the words he had put down, he slipped into the question why not, why not now, why not immediately? He felt good now, in another interval between the hot and cold swings of the fever. He would go out, take a taxi, and go searching to see if Juana had come back.

Searching for his wallet he made up his mind it would be unwise, now that he had finally resigned, to spend money on long taxi trips. He would have to be careful from now on. He would take a slow walk; no buses ever ran from Link Road to the Cantonment, and such a walk could be a good, slow way to see the city in his own time.

The moment he stepped out of his room he met his uncle Foli. The man was attempting to smile, but the only thing visible on his face was a tight kind of fear of something unfinished.

"Did you sleep at all, Baako?" his uncle asked with the smile.

"Yes."

"Not very soundly, then?"

"Uncle Foli, I slept."

"Hmm."

Baako was moving toward the porch door when his uncle hurried ahead of him, blocked the doorway with his body, and, looking warily at him, called out past him into the house, "Korankye! Kofi!" The noise of hurrying feet reached Baako from behind. Gathering in the pit of his right arm, a rill of sweat slid down his side. It was cold. He turned to see the advancing shape of Korankye the Hunchback.

"I didn't know Korankye had come," he said.

"Yes, Korankye is here," his uncle answered.

"Master, it's me," Korankye said. He came closer, looking downward all the time, like an embarrassed criminal.

"I see," said Baako. He felt weak. Behind Korankye two other men had approached, silent, with the air of men awaiting an important, secret order. Baako looked at them, then at his uncle, and asked, "Who are these others?"

"Friends, Baako," his uncle answered. "They came to help. Baako, you must rest."

He was feeling closed in standing there with Korankye and the two strangers behind him, looking into his uncle's eyes in front. It was a strange turn his uncle's answer had taken, he thought, but he did not feel like standing now and asking any more questions. He moved forward, expecting his uncle would step aside to let him pass, but all the man did was ask him, "Where are you going?" Stopped in this way, Baako looked up into his uncle's face and just stared, not knowing what he could say; and his uncle continue, "Is it something you may be needing? Korankye will go out and get it for you, Baako."

"I'm going out myself," he said.

"No, Baako," his uncle said. This was a kind voice, with such a confusing message. But he had heard right. "You're sick. You must rest here till we take you to get help." In Baako's ears the words did not come to an end; they flowed on and picked up leftover sounds from yesterday. Nothing really, something, something, nothing, something something something. He closed his eyes, hoping the panic in him would not rise so uncontrollably fast.

"I must go," he said quietly. Immediately he pushed forward, pressing his uncle to one side, making enough space for his body to get through. Someone was holding his arm in a rather gentle grip from behind. He twisted it free and said to the four men behind him, "Leave me alone. I've done nothing to any of you. Don't touch me." But they were moving toward him, their arms reaching out to catch hold of him. He turned from them, thinking he would go out and leave them in the yard, but at that moment Korankye bounded past him with a little cry like a moan, reached the gate first and swung it shut, pulling the bolt on it. The others, not so fast, he could hear panting behind him. He had only a second to think, and almost before the thought had entered his mind he turned sharply to the right, leaped when he reached the wall and clutched the top of it, hurled his weight upward with no break in speed, and the next moment dropped down the other side, free from pursuit. He began walking to the street. The voices he heard from within sounded far away and muffled, and for some moments he imagined they had nothing to do with him.

"Lord, he jumped!"

"Hold him!"

"Over the wall!"

"Oh Christ!"

"Yes, he did!"

"He jumped!"

"He jumped!"

He ran to keep free, but inside his head voices from the night before told him he had come to the end this time, he might as well give up. He did not have to turn to know he was in danger. On the road before him a small group of boys watching two play gutterball turned to look at him, took a moment making up its mind and then picked up stones from the roadside to throw at him. He ducked in mid-stride to avoid the stones, but they seemed to fly all at once and one of them, thrown so fast it looked to be floating on low pads of air, gathered speed and hit him straight on the hard cap of his raised left knee. He heard noises that now made too much sudden sense.

"Stop him!"

"Hold him!"

"Don't let him goooo!"

"Get him!"

"Thiiiiiief!"

In the shouting and the running there was no time to stop and see what damage had been done. The children who had thrown their stones were bending to pick up new ones. He twisted quickly left, shrank his body to push it through a hole cut in a thornbush hedge, then came upon red-brown, uneven ground, running across patches of dry grass. The noise behind him was loud, and it was wilder now. His head felt light and his mouth was dry, its saliva thickened into one minute spot of bitter phlegm. He did not think of his tiredness, he could not think of it anymore, there was so much of it in every part of him. But he made the effort, and when he had achieved concentration the idea that rose from his fear made his muscles freeze. At this rate they could follow him till he dropped exhausted and then they would do whatever it was they were running after him straining to do. In the direction he was running he could think of nothing to give him safety. Better to stop while he had some breath left; the four men from his home might choose to explain, after all.

He stopped. A small shower of stones fell not far from him, and a couple hit him, then there were no more. The first of the pursuers were near, and now that he was theirs they were hesitating about taking him. Two or three of the children who had followed him, however, seemed entirely free of the general diffidence, intent only on reaching him with new stones and their hands. But before they could get to him a frightened shout stilled them, its meaning petrifying them each for long moments at the point he'd reached.

"Stay far from him. His bite will make you also maaaaad!"

To this another, closer voice added in sage, quiet tones, "The same thing happens if he should scratch you."

What succeeded the hearing of those sounds was the clearest daylight, he thought, the neatest sunlight he had ever seen. It was as if there was absolutely nothing, not even air, between him and anyone, any other thing around, and all the distance to the sky was filled with light. Before him he saw the children fall back into the adults following, precipitately at first, but with more ease when they saw he was not running back after them. He walked slowly, and they moved back a little faster, keeping a gently increasing distance betweeen themselves and him. Now that he could look at his pursuers, he saw there was no one there he recognized. He had lived here a year, knowing nobody around. But then as the thought took speed he knew this was true not of the area alone, but of the whole city. He knew no friends, no one. The people he had worked with at Ghanavision he had not known so well that he could think of them as friends at a time like this. Juana, of course. But she was away, or perhaps was just arriving from a tiring voyage. But in the area around, no one.

He would stop a car once he got to the road. Someone might understand enough to pick him up and drive him away from this crowd, somewhere where he could take a cool drink at last and try himself to understand fully the things that had happened in the night and this morning. When he reached the road he stood beside it thinking, the crowd forming a scattered ring around him. A red Vauxhall was the first to come. He tried to stop it but the owner of it accelerated like a frightened man. A white Peugeot followed, and also left him in the street waving in the clear air. A small gray cloud hazed over the sunlight momentarily. When it was gone Baako felt the chill in his bones again, but outside he was sweating; the shirt he had on clung to his back, and sweat-stained drawers irritated the skin of his buttocks. The pursuers around him were no longer so careful about keeping their distance from him, though no one facing him was willing to venture too near. He felt calm in a strange, distracted way.

A Mercedes Benz came by next, new and smoothly black. He did not raise a hand to stop it, but planted his body in the dead middle of the road, forcing the car to a halt. Now he went left to the window to talk to the other within, but the moment he left the road clear the car eased forward with a careful slowness. Baako could not see the face within, but inside his head there were images of people who should be riding like this past him now.

"Listen, look!" he shouted, hoping this time the owner would really stop his car. But it went by, the wheels moving slowly, inexorably.

"Brempong!" His shout was a numb question, unanswered in the end. He did not let the car go. He held on to the vertical bar between the front and the back windows, ran alongside the owner inside driving straight ahead, and did not let go until the speed of the car began to lift his trailing legs behind him, bringing them scraping back on the surface of the road. When he lost his grip he heard the car's oiled acceleration and the noises of the crowd.

"Jesus! He killed himself."

"No. But he almost did."

"But what thing is this?"

"Some enemy he made has done him this."

"It was himself, they say."

"Books."

"Ah, yes. Books."

"Books."

No one seemed able to make up his mind what ought to be done, and from the road he heard the confusion around him worsening, until a high cry cut off all the other voices; the voice he recognized as Araba's and the recognition disturbed him.

"Do something, please. Do something now, before he kills himself."

The confused murmur continued, however, after a little pause; there were questions asked, and some answers.

"His sister, yes."

In a while Araba's sobs subsided and she said in the uncertain silence, "Tie him up."

He did not feel so weak any more. He turned to look at his sister. Her eyes were sunken in her head with sorrow. They looked as if they had been red from birth. Things filled with grief, and a certain anger, but now he couldn't think for whom, against whom. When he rose from the street he saw two men approaching. He did not know where they had gone, but in their hands they carried ropes, and a third one followed after them with shorter lengths of twine.

For a long time, an hour perhaps, it seemed to him, he jumped and ran in circles to avoid the ropes thrown at him.

"Tire him," a man had said, breathing hard. The others had taken lengths of rope and slowly aimed them at his legs to snare him, watching him jump to get out of the way. Near the end he was sweating, and the fever shook him while he jumped and shifted. There was nothing between him and those around, not even hate from them or from him, just their steady determination to take him and his slowing efforts to escape, going nowhere. He grew tired and was ready to sit down when one man aiming well threw his rope and caught his ankles, yanked the tight fiber and brought him down. He was not worried about struggling with his pursuers any more, but he was full of a wonder that threatened to turn into fear. He had landed on his back. When his head cleared he looked up to see the sky; it was the color of one unending sheet of fresh aluminum.

Now the others were quick with the speed of fearful men about to be released from their fear. While his wrists were being bound, a man in sandals was called to stand on his fingers so he would not scratch while the knots binding his legs and arms were made tight enough to keep him from breaking loose again. The fiber of the twine ate toward the wrist bones, cutting his flesh.

"If you could loosen this . . ." he began. But it seemed they had stopped looking at him, or listening to anything he might say.

Men took him home, taking care not to come near his nails or head while carrying him, and laid him down in the yard. The crowd came in and stood around, and since they had put him down on his back he could see them shake their heads and talk. It was a litany of sorrow they were saying, all of them, and to him now they seemed full of strangely twisted truths and unaccountable lies, all flowing together in a steam he could do nothing to stop.

"It was books, they say."

"And he was clever in school."

"A been-to, returned only a year ago. His mother waited a long time, and now this happens to her."

"He was very quiet."

"Is it true that he was a graduate?"

"Yes, and a been-to."

"We saw him walking to take the bus every morning, so we were not so sure."

"A graduate all right. Hundred percent."

"Strange, he didn't have a car."

"They could at least have given him a bungalow."

"Strange."

"Strange."

Once he heard his grandmother Naana's voice, asking, "What have you done to him? What has Baako done to you? Where is he?" But no one answered her, and after a while he thought someone must have silenced her.

A little green bus backed into the yard and the men heaved him onto its metal floor. On the trip out he could not raise his head to look out and see where the bus was going. There was a chink in the metal below, but through it there was only the rushing tar of the roadway, smooth, unchanging. Once, forgetting himself, he pleaded to be let down and had his head pressed closer to the floor. They let him down inside the yard of the Asylum. A nurse in blue came and looked at him, ordered the men with him to free his hands if he had not been violent with anyone, and said pensively, "The way he came in, he will have to go to the Acute Ward."

He woke up feeling the warmth of the cement beneath him. The sun was still strong, but it was going west, about to slide behind the high cross of the Roman Catholic Cathedral on the bell tower rising above the wires on the Asylum wall. Two other madmen detached themselves from a larger group. One of them had a Bible, and from it he read out loud an endless stream of inspired words. The other followed. When the two reached him they stopped as though at some secret signal passed between them, stared curiously at him, shook their heads in unison, smiled and walked slowly backwards away from him. He looked above their heads and his eyes were caught by the purple flowers of a plant whose stem had climbed the roof in front. He felt extremely lucky.

10 : Efua

ONE REPEATED THOUGHT took his mind and sped through his head like frames carrying an unchanging accusation: right, right, they're right, right, right. In the beginning there was a mother's expectant, happy smile and a sweet voice telling the arrived one about a mansion fit for him. Like a newborn fool he had seen no need to go off into huge mansions and inflate himself to fill the space. Had he thought then that such refusals would be understood, or had he understood but chosen to push under the mute contemplation and the mother's following question, asked with that good smile that still held out the hope of peace, "The eagle does not want to soar?" That was truly fearsome, they were right, right, right about his willingness to look for something not so far from themselves, this nothingness they were dying to leave behind. That was perverse and they were right again, right, right. A certain haughtiness would have been salutary, something closer to the spirit of his hosts beyond the horizon would have reassured everyone and saved him from provoking his own doom.

The arrived one had been invited to sit down, rest his tired soul and let a hungry body fill itself. The three cocks selected and brought by Fifi for the feast were white, so what could have been better? The drinks were to be the imported kind, and the happy tongues around struggled with strange European names calling out the foods, struggled and conquered, and then the foolish one asked why all these fripperies, and after that the laughter lost its joy and there was no feast, nothing, as he had so blindly told the laughing ones, nothing to celebrate.

Right, right, right. That refusal of ritual joy certainly spoke to them of some horrifying inner shrinking, of a soul measuring everything, leaving nothing flying loose for even hangers-on and close ones with hopes too far out for their lonely reach. If still-creeping lianas could talk, what would they say to their self-stunted tree? What could anyone expect, puncturing every inflation of hope, destroying bubbles that were not only beautiful but also real to their makers: "But couldn't you have got one for yourself?"

And Efua was right to think of the returned one as fruit, ripe fruit of her womb. Seeing the other fruit grow riper, watching hers turn green and hard and hurtful to the open consuming mouth, she was right. What had she done wrong that all her hope should be so harshly torn? He would always stand outside, against himself, trying to find out why.

Then again all was clear now, and it was too late anyway. It did not have any of the form of a dream, just a daylight remembrance of words said and events that had happened far apart, now no longer separate but pushed into each other, a compressed reel entering him with a new, clear meaning. There had also been warnings from Naana, and the old woman had been right in her blindness: he had heard her but always in the end he had ignored her, just as he had missed the signs flowing out to him from his mother. She was right.

"Come," his mother Efua had said, surprising him that Sunday morning.

"Where?"

"You come with me. There's something I have to show you."

He followed her down that same road, walked with her to the Winneba junction and sat with her waiting for a bus. He was impatient but she laughed almost all the time that morning, telling him not to let the waiting make him angry.

"There are annoying things in this life here," she laughed, "but we must find our happiness all the same." She looked at him and smiled, waiting for something, but he did not feel like talking and she went on by herself. "I made a decision today. I'm cleaning my soul."

"What was in it?" he asked her.

"Dirt," she said, so calmly that he laughed. "True. It was like before I went to the prophet. I was cursing you in my heart, though, not crying for you."

"And which of my sins . . ."

"Not sins," she said. "It was me. I was waiting for you to see this world here and live in it, knowing where the roads are and the walls. It was as if I was afraid you'd destroy yourself."

"Doesn't sound like a curse."

"But it was. You just don't know how it was. I was wanting you to do some things. Now my wishes have disappeared, and I'm finding happiness."

"Did you go back to the prophet?"

"No," she said. "He was angry that I stopped going to him the same month you arrived. He doesn't like people who have faith only when they want things. He's very strange, my prophet, I don't go to him anymore."

"You found someone else," he said.

"Something filled my mind and I understood," she said, turning slightly to look up the road. "I was like a child, not looking at myself but wishing you would see the world. The thing that filled my mind suddenly was that you were part of my world, one of my walls."

"What's that mean?"

"You won't understand. We come to walls in life, all the time. If we try to break them down we destroy ourselves. I was wanting you to break down and see the world here, before I saw you yourself were a wall."

"That's a strange thing to be," he said.

"Once I saw that I was free to decide — to leave you alone. That's how I began my soulcleaning." She smiled. "But there was something I had hidden from you. That was like hiding it from myself, in a way."

No bus came but a small *tro-tro* bus on its way to Swedru stopped for them and the mate dropped them where Efua told him to stop. Where they turned off, the tarred road branched sharply to the right, away from their path, after a hundred yards, giving place to raw, stony laterite earth. At the fork there was a new gate of iron and barbed wire behind which a shiny road stretched out, turning in its last half up a hill with a large, almost-finished house on it.

"That's the Special Commissioner Kunkumfi's house," Efua said. "He would have finished it long ago, too. But every time he travels to Europe or America he sees a new style he wants to add. Look at it. Isn't it beautiful?"

Past rains had torn gullies into the surface of the dirt road they were on, leaving jagged slate edges and pieces of chipped stone exposed, so that they had to walk carefully. Once he almost stepped on a broken board lying in the middle of the road with two rusty, twisted nails sticking out of it. The road opened out into a large, cleared space beyond which there was only a faint path in the undergrowth. It was a clearing that seemed filled with broken things and with unfinished work stopped violently for some sudden reason, leaving wrenched, jagged edges that gave the eye a feeling of being grated against a thousand snapped fractions of things. Someone had planted rows of little trees not too long ago, but only stumps of the growing plants were left now, with an occasional leaf also half chewed through by some wandering animal. Two crude wooden machines lay broken, their boards eaten in places by termites. Some of the blocks they had already made had fallen apart, but there was still a pile leaning sideways, waiting for the ruin of a final fall. Next to them were cracked stones brought from a granite quarry, and a larger heap of sand now mixed with blown red dust.

"Come," Efua said with her smile.

The house was unfinished, barely begun, really. The foundation had all been laid, and it was huge; but the wall was high only on one small side. Everywhere else it was so low and incomplete it was possible to see through the hollow bricks right down to the foundation in the earth. Far out in the high distance a jet plane passed, silver white itself and trailing a white mist, growing smaller in its flight with a sound just slipping beyond hearing, and more disturbing because of that. Efua stood completely still, her face raised after the plane.

"That always made me think of you," she said after the plane was gone. "It must make you so different to have flown, looking at us all crawling down below. I used to think of your coming when I saw a plane. Now all I think is I won't ever fly."

Efua went in through a door space. He followed, thinking but not asking why she had brought him to this unfinished place.

"The entryway, the hall, and a kitchen over there," she said in a stream of words that had come quickly together even then. "These rooms were warm like a good, deep dream." She went by a pile of pipes, unused but also twisted, already old with verdigris and rust, beneath a tube sticking out of the floor, a future shower, perhaps. A white toilet bowl lay there too, its enamel cracked in some accidental fall. Nothing but low walls followed, then a room where copper wiring stuck out of gray flex with red sleeves showing. And she had had questions for him, what had he answered then? "You've gone so far up, everyone of us cripples here beneath must look so foolish to you. But don't laugh at us. It's admiration. If our souls are so dirty it's because of the desire to fly too." And then a long silence in which she turned round and round looking at everything in the unfinished house like a woman saying a farewell to a lover destroyed, and that beautiful laughing voice again: "It isn't so hard, the soulcleaning."

Unable to keep down his thoughts about the strange, unfinished walls, he looked at her coming from the other end of the house and said what he was feeling, "Doesn't it look like a huge, extravagant thing from a dream somewhere?"

Even then she'd laughed, his mother Efua, without much sound, but perhaps that was deliberate, to bring out the visual beauty of that laugh too.

"That is the last thing in my soulcleaning, Baako," she said. "These stones and the sand, they were mine. I started all this, thinking I was building something you would come and not find too small. I was hoping you would come back to me, take joy in the thing I had begun but will never end, and finish it. That was the meaning of my curse on you. Forgive me. Now that we have both come and seen this, I won't accuse you anymore. Again I'm a mother, confessing what strange feelings you've sent through me. It's over now, Baako. Can you understand? We can go home now." And still that happy laugh, all the way to the bus stop, waiting in the sun for whatever would come.

11 : Iwu

ALL WAS DARK and comfortable inside the Acute Ward at night. He lay on his back feeling the hardness of the wallet he still had with him against his right buttock. In the warmth inside the ward he was sweating, but the cement floor felt through his wet shirt had a soothing coolness. He could not think how many days he'd been wearing these clothes, nor how long he'd been in the ward, and it didn't matter anyhow; outside he would have no clear idea of any place left to go. And yet out there, apart from the others, should be Naana and Juana. Women destroying, women saving. Every bit of sense hurried to destroy itself in headlong explosion. Ocran too, but the idea of him brought uncertain thoughts; besides, it was too hard trying to shape ideas of where they all might be at this time. The only quiet was in a confusion so full that thinking would not lead out of it but into a dizzier whirl, and the one way to make peace with it was to give up and let all struggle go.

He couldn't sleep anymore. The night sounds from the others rose and fell steadily. He shifted so he could draw out the wallet. It still felt smooth to his fingers, though it had become bent to the mould of his buttock. In his pocket it had felt warm, but in his hands it was cool leather. With a far-of curiosity he opened it and felt in it, seeing nothing. His fingers touched no money, only bits of paper he couldn't remember ever having gathered. One of them, though also thin, was firm to the touch and shone in the darkness with a soft green radiance. He was almost sure he had thrown the big man Brempong's card away, though. But trying to think of his life made the whirl start again inside his head. Near the heavy door another madman roared fiercely in some sleepy struggle and continued afterward muttering against the foes he had kept with him in his mind.

Naana, Juana, Ocran. There had been the other, the child that was to have grown to become him, but they had killed him, or had he also helped in the murder after all? You are so sudden, Naana had told him, but that was because she had given up. Save him was what she had said, and then he had done things suddenly, too late, and some things he should have done he'd never done.

They'd put the baby in a new cradle lined with deep-colored blue, gold, red and green *kente* and put him out there on the porch, a square of the morning sunlight falling on one side of a wide brass pan next to him. The fan stood behind the cradle, something else he had tried not to understand that day. They came in magnificent Sunday groups, the guests, their splendor making it impossible for Efua to keep from smiling and going beyond the gate to look at the line of cars before the ceremony could start.

It was a purely unreasonable situation he himself was in, or perhaps he had already lost track of reasons. He was to be the Master of Ceremonies — everyone seemed intent on calling him that name, that he could remember, yet not one face there bore the slightest trace of mockery. Efua stood on tiptoe on the highest step of the porch still gazing over the wall, checking in her mind how far the line of cars was reaching down the street, and her smile lingered after her eyes came back to look at the people in the yard.

This was a rich crowd of guests, too, sitting at first like a picture already taken. Woolen suits, flashing shoes, important crossed legs, bright rings showing on intertwined fingers held in front of restful bellies, an authentic cold-climate overcoat from Europe or America held traveler-fashion over an arm, five or six waistcoats, silken ties and silver clasps, and a magnificent sane man in a university gown reigning over four admiring women in white lace covershirts on new dumas cloth; long, twinkling earrings, gold necklaces, quick-shining wristwatches, a great rich splendor stifling all these people in the warmth of a beautiful day — but that was only an addition to the wonder: the sweat called forth new white handerchiefs brought out with a happy flourish, spreading perfume underneath the mango trees. The hunchback himself was in royal *kente*, brilliant as a painting set against the gate, looking anguished after cars that came by and didn't stop to let out more glistening dignitaries for him to welcome to the feast.

Against all that happiness there was a solitary fool walking into the midst of things wearing only reasonable clothes, a shirt and a northtern *batakari* over a pair of shorts.

"At least wear something decent."

The clown, being blind, had had the confidence to be impatient with the entreaty, asking, "What's wrong with this?" and watched pure surprise slide into an overbrave public smile on his mother's face as she moved into the celebrating crowd holding a beer tray packed with glasses and bottles.

A fragrant young woman walked up to the porch to get another tray, stopped before the clown with eyebrows raised in some hidden, exquisite conspiratorial question, her face so close her breath was a warm sweet suspended mixture of spirits, some strange perfume and a live desire, and she was holding her lips open and her eyes a quarter or so closed, the whole of her person shaped now into a held-in invitation driving her question into him.

"Ei, mister been-to. Is that how quickly you forget those who love you? I know you don't even remember my name now, mister been-to."

"Christina."

"Yes, mister been-to. You promised to come and take me for a cool ride one day and here you've hidden from me for months already."

"I haven't been hiding."

Christina laughed at him, her sound liquid, pure and effortless joy. "I do believe you're scared now," she said. "Look, I'm just a woman after you. Promise again you're going to give me that long ride soon. Tomorrow?"

"I never promised."

"Don't pretend you can't remember. Soon as your car arrived, you told me. My witnesses are God, Feef and myself. You know I could sue you for breach of promise, mister been-to, oh truly. You've caused me to dream of us two ever since. See, my eyes are sleepy still."

The clown laughed, hoping to wash everything away, but the beauty before him wouldn't let go that easily.

"I mean it, mister been-to. You — broke — your — promise." She touched him on the cheek, lightly.

"I told you I wasn't going to have a car," he said.

"Yes, oh yes, mister been-to, you told me. And like the new baby, I believed you eh?"

"That's the truth, you know."

She laughed. "Look, throats shouldn't stay dry at a festival. Let me take the drinks down, but don't run away. I want to talk to you. I'll find you anyway."

She stepped down from the porch, going among the guests with her tray of drinks; when she got to Fifi's seat she spun in a pretty high-life step, a swift little circle that did not break the balance of her tray, and when she gave the drink to Fifi she also leaned to whisper in his ear; whatever she said made him smile and look up in the direction of the clown on the porch.

Kwesi started the radiogram playing loud and full before walking out himself to join the guests, smiling in his uncertain way, answering congratulations, shaking hands.

"Ei, the happy father."

"His soul has brought him luck."

"This child should bring wealth."

"And happiness."

"He will, that is certain."

"Happiness to you, father."

"And prosperity too."

The way it was then, the talk out in the yard was unrestrained, but its freedom did not fight the music; it just rode on a pleasant cushion of smoother sound, completing the morning's mood.

Naana appeared in the doorway and stood there looking collected and very intent. She smiled when he went and took her hand.

"Ah, Baako, it was you I was searching for," she said. He gave her a chair near the low veranda wall he'd been sitting on. "I would have found you, too," the blind woman continued.

"How, Naana?"

"You're smiling, your voice says you don't believe me. But I can always find you. I was listening for a silence in this noise. I knew you'd be there." She laughed.

"You want something to drink?"

"Yes," she said, "but not a lot. Just pass me your glass from time to time." She took a slow draught. "This is cool and it feels good on the tongue, Baako. Still, I'm not forgetting my anger. You should have saved the child."

"He's all right, Naana."

"You talk like a child, yourself. Where have they put him?"

"They made a thing to put him in, Naana. He's just here, lying in it."

"My mind can see him, lying in state now."

"He's all right, Naana, really. He's been very quiet."

"Hmm." The old woman seemed to be listening again, to something on the other side of the present sounds. "Did they pour a libation before starting this drinking? I heard nothing, neither the silence nor the words."

"There was no libation, Naana."

"Do not play with me, Baako. You made my heart jump."

"It's true, there was none."

She sighed. "Great friend, they have taken to forgetting the ancestors themselves. They do not look to those gone before, and they do not see the child. Where are their eyes, then?"

"Naana, it's a new festival."

"So it seems. But, Baako, you're young. Have you no anger?"

"What would I do?"

"How he talks like a clever elder. A question to answer my question." She smiled. "I hear your mother's laughter."

"She's coming this way."

"Now, Baako, now!" Efua said, coming close enough for a fierce whisper.

"Now what?" he asked.

"The collection, Baako."

"Oh, I thought that came after everything."

"No, now," Efua said. "They've had something to drink and they're waiting for the food."

"Fine," he said. "Naana, I'll be with you in a moment." He jumped down.

"The money goes in the brass pan," Efua said.

He walked past the baby's cradle, stooped to take up the brass pan, and stood on the top step of the porch looking down into the container. The music went dead and the crowd grew quiet. At the moment when he should have had the utmost poise, the clown felt a heavy uneasiness.

"Well," he began, "there's this thing here, the brass pan in my hand. I'm going to put it down here for all those who'd like to put some money in it." Relieved he placed the pan down and raised his arm to wipe the sweat on his forehead with his sleeve. Then he turned, his intention being to go and get the music turned up again. But in front of him he saw Efua's advancing face, unbelieving, baffled. She asked no questions then, though. She simply walked into the waiting silence behind him, lifted the brass pan so it shone where the light hit it, and raised her voice:

"Friends, ladies, gentlemen,

"It's time now for each and every person present on this happy occasion to rise up and give a generous donation in appreciation of the birth of this happy child. I will call on you, and you will all come here to the front and give from the bottom of your heart. I will call the honorable VIP guests first, the rest later. First . . . the honorable Mr. Charles Winston Churchill Kessie, Protocol Branch, Ministry of External Affairs, please step forward and show your appreciation."

An overjoyed little man stepped solemnly forward, the black of his face tinged with a little of the suit's blue, a white handkerchief showing from his coat pocket like the echo of his smile. He walked to the brass pan, took out his wallet from an inner pocket, extracted five separate cedi notes and allowed them to drift gingerly downward to the bottom of the pan.

"Three, four, five!" Efua counted, and the clownish thing in him then made him think she was like a female referee. "The big man from Protocol has given five. Let's clap for him!" The clapping ended, the little dignitary turned to go, and Efua continued. "Now I will call on . . . Mrs. Kessie. Let the wife of the big man show what she too can do!"

The big man on his way to his seat turned suddenly like an animal freshly shot, surprise twisting his mouth. But a moment later he had recovered from this shock, and reaching once more into the inner pocket he pulled out his wallet and gave it unopened to his wife on her sullen way up to the porch. There was a sigh so sharp it could not have come from one woman alone, but from many catching breath in unison; and then a hushed noise followed.

"What's wrong, Baako?" his grandmother asked.

"Nothing," he said.

"But there's a kind of noise."

True. He looked at the crowd and saw hands in furtive haste passing and receiving money, then just as suddenly the movement ended and there was no noise of rustling paper and hard coins, just voices whispering again.

"Wise men were slipping money to their wives to give," he said.

"Four cedis!" Efua shouted. "Let's all clap for her. The big man's wife has made us proud with four . . . Inspector Duncan Afum . . . Police Inspector Duncan Afum, your turn now. Show your powers, Inspector . . ." Efua put the pan down to wipe her face with a handkerchief, then turned to look at the baby in the cradle, shook her head from side to side and immediately switched on the fan, turning the air current directly against the cradle.

"What do they want with this wind machine?" his grandmother asked, spitting over the low wall.

"To cool the baby," the clown said.

Naana laughed. "To boast, more likely," she said. "If I know them, they've got him shrouded in rich clothes and now they turn this wind on him."

Above the fan's steady noise Efua continued to call out the donor's names. Watching, he felt himself receding physically from the scene, a clown looking at a show turned inside out. The thing that brought him out of his suspension was the baby's weeping. It began as though the child were looking for a way to laugh, and the crying kept a playful sound minutes after it had started. But then a full, terrifying shout burst from the cradle, and in the same instant the clown came off his wall and bounded the few steps to the cradle. Trying to stop the fan he fumbled, the buttons he pushed making the machine run faster. So he took the thing by its stem and yanked in anger once. Sparks flew out in a small shower where the cord snapped at the base of the fan, and the clown let the heavy thing drop into the brass pan, still turning, scattering the gathered notes.

The confusion brought Araba out, smiling feebly, a hand on her abdomen, still visibly in pain. She did not seem able to say anything; she just took the child and went back in, leaving her mother Efua looking vacantly out into the yard, standing upright among the scattered notes.

The guests, those who waited, ate in silence when the ritual food was served. At the end only the gowned graduate seemed to have any joy left in him. He tried to raise a general song, but he himself could manage but one line which he repeated several times, hoping perhaps to remember the rest that way:

> For he's a joll-ley good fell-low . . .
> For he's a joll-ley good fell-low . . .

When the yard was empty his grandmother called his name.

"It was too sudden, whatever you did," she said. "Everything is wrong now."

*

Three weeks after the child was buried Efua asked for help and the clown asked her what for.

"The time has come to put an announcement in the papers. For the baby."

"Why?"

"I can't understand your questions, Baako. You know we should write a farewell in the papers."

"For the baby, how?"

"What?"

"Seems to me we're still going for the show."

"Baako, I'm tired. I need your help. Can you write the farewell announcement? It's only a poem."

"I wouldn't know how to do it."

"You refuse to help us then."

*

Looking at the newspaper, he had been slow to recognize the photo of the child. At first it looked like all the others, then the sight of the fan in the background made him stare at the words.

> A month ago today, dear angel,
> Cruel Death took you from our hands.
> The blow was hard, the tears bitter.
> You will never leave our hearts
> Till once again we are all united
> In the bosom of our Lord.
> Rest in Peace, dear Child,

Bye Bye.

CHIEF MOURNERS: Mrs. Efua Onipa, Certified Teacher,
Radiantway International School.
Mr. Baako Onipa, BA, Senior Officer,
Ghanavision.
Mr. Kwesi Baiden, Technical Staff,
Volta Aluminium Company, Tema.

12 : Obra

SHE FOUND HIM sitting on the ground in the walled space outside the Acute Ward, leaning back on his elbows and looking up above the west wall. She turned to look for the thing holding his gaze but all there was was the tower of the Catholic cathedral. She sat by him on the ground; two inmates came curiously closer and stopped a few steps away, just looking. She had a moment's small fear that he had not recognized her — he sat so still — and it made her wish, like a woman praying, that the long silences and brief, slanted abortions of contact would fade completely into the past and she could talk to him again, renew the interest he had lost in holding on. He spoke first this time.

"How's Skido?"

"Skido?"

"You saw him on the way. He wasn't like me. He was bringing all the cargo and he shouldn't have died, not like that."

"Baako, who's Skido?"

"You know. I know you know. You're trying to protect him, that's good. Don't be afraid now. I'm a friend, and he's gone." He smiled before sinking into another bottomless silence.

"I talked again to the Doctor here," she said.

"He's all right."

"He's ready now to have you moved to a transitional ward."

"I'm all right."

"Baako, can't you tell me what happened?"

"Ask the others. They're right all the time, you see."

"Your family? I've been talking to them, but there was something no one seemed to understand. The old woman came to talk to me once when I went in. I didn't understand her, but I think she said they tried to kill you."

"Ah, Naana. Did you know she called me sudden? She was right, too."

"What happened, Baako?"

"They told you the truth. I forgot the cargo — swallowed it."

"Baako, this is me."

"Your name is Juana. You're my friend Skido. You must protect yourself. You can't go back anywhere with nothing in your hands. It's a mistake — not a mistake, an insult."

"Will you come and stay with me, as soon as you're out?"

"I'm all right. Protect yourself. There's one town we never went to: Bibiani."

"I was on a trip there once, before we met."

"No one told you the meaning of that name."

"I didn't think of it. I thought it was just another name for a town."

"Let me break it for you. *Beebi ara ni.*"

"Wait a moment. Somewhere, no, everywhere . . . is this."

"This is everywhere."

A nurse came round with a cooler of water and some pills. Baako shook his head, but before the nurse could get impatient Juana took the pills and a cup of the water and the nurse went off.

"It's the way you were brought in here, I'm told," she said. "The staff thinks there must have been something very wrong."

"They're right. I'm crazy."

"The Doctor says he'll let you out when you respond to treatment. He just means he wants you to be quiet and take that medicine. Don't argue with anyone. You can't win."

"That's something I should have known too. Outside."

"What really happened?"

"You don't have to be told. The cargo, that's it, really. Do you think the traveler should have come back just like that? Who needs what's in a head?"

"You're accusing yourself again. You're not a criminal. You were trying to do something. It isn't wrong just because people say it is."

"Arrogance. It's all arrogance without the others, isn't it?"

She searched in herself for something that might make sense, but there was nothing she could herself believe in, nothing that wouldn't just be the high flight of the individual alone, escaping the touch of life around him. That way she knew there was only annihilation. Yet here she knew terrible dangers had been lying in wait the other way — other kinds of annihilation. How could she find the thing to break down his despair when she had never conquered hers? There would be no meaning in offering him a chance to swing from present hopelessness to a different flavor of despair.

She took his hand and held it, caressing it; a fullness of affection she had been unable to let out in words broke through and took complete possession of her. He seemed to have felt it too, and moved closer against her. The resistance that had been so strong in his words was gone, and his body next to hers felt totally willing. He was crying again.

"Come and stay," she said. "Stay with me when you come. As long as you want."

He smiled. "That medicine," he said, nodding, "I thought they were giving it to me to drive me crazier."

"It's good medicine," she said.

She gave him the pills when he asked for them, and after he had taken them he rested his head in her lap and she stroked his arms, neither of them saying anything.

Ocran came in with a nurse and stood looking at them before sitting down next to her.

"How are you, Onipa?" Ocran asked.

"The same," Baako said. "But they'll change the criminal."

"You look more like a lover to me."

"Juana is my only friend."

"You count me out then?"

"Teachers I don't know about. Turning them into friends, that's difficult. Something hard always remains. But I've done wrong anyway. You shouldn't be coming too close to me."

She saw Ocran's look, and guessed what he was thinking, but she turned her head away, and the cathedral tower caught her eyes once again.

"What you said the last time confused me," Ocran was saying. "I wondered how you came to think that. But I thought of it, and I think I know. I wasn't honest, I didn't look far enough back at myself." He took the cup and drank the water Baako had left in it. "I went the same way, too. You know, when you know what you want to do, there's no sense in setting other people up in your mind to pass judgment on you."

"They're there, though," Baako said.

"Move them out. You can't do anything else without first clearing them out of yourself. You can't even see clearly the thing you yourself need to do."

"It seemed to me there was nothing to be done outside of them, the others."

"In the end it's true," Ocran said. "But if you make it immediately . . . if you do that you end up accusing yourself. Did you really mean what you said last time, about wanting to be like that man in the Bank, and the Productivity bureaucrat — what the hell is his name?"

"Brempong."

"Well, do you?"

"I have to be. I wouldn't be here if I'd known that. That wouldn't be a crime."

"You can't be like them. You make me think of Akosua Russell when you talk of those people. You know you aren't that way."

"If I made up my mind it was the right way to be . . ."

"Look," Ocran said sharply, "those people didn't choose to be like that. If they couldn't be like that, they'd be nothing."

"I don't know," Baako said.

"You know. Don't stop thinking, Onipa. You have a good mind; don't be afraid to use it. Stop thinking you've done people wrong. Nobody cares, anyway. If these people had your talent, they wouldn't want to be that way. They wouldn't *need* to."

"They're useful."

"If that's all the usefulness you can think of. We all have relatives who want us to be like your Brempong — get them things that shout they're rich, they're powerful. But you don't have time for that nonsense. The country's full of people dying to look down on everybody else."

"I've thought of that," said Baako. "It's most natural."

"Think again. Look well at all the people needing to have things to set them above people. Position, power, cars, wigs, houses, money. If they lost those things they'd get sick with their own emptiness. You have something to do. Forget about the rest and get on with it."

"It's not so easy, that decision to disappoint . . ."

"The relatives, you keep talking about them. I suppose you're right in not blaming them for wanting things. But it's senseless to get sick because you can't help them get what they want. There'd be no end to these wants once you started destroying your life to satisfy them. They're not interested in your hopes, have you thought of that? In a way there's no danger to you, personally, from those like your Bank friend and that Brempong you talk of. They want things, and they're worked out a way to get them. The ones you have to be careful of are the impotent ones. They also want the same things but don't know how to cheat their way to them. You're just someone they'd like to use to get what they want. Is that what you want to be? Something your relatives use to get things?"

"It's the cargo," Baako said. "After all, there's no way not to use people, growing."

Ocran looked from Baako to Juana, incomprehension on his face. She did not want the thread broken, so she said, "It can be a terrifying conflict, if you see the need to help the relatives, though, and also to do something useful in a larger sense. There are two communities, really, and they don't coincide. It's not easy to work out priorities."

"We still have to choose," Ocran said, sighing. "Pardon me, I talk like a brute, but we have to choose. Yourself, Baako, your problems are different from your relatives'. You have a fullness you need to bring out. It's not an emptiness you need to cover up with things. You're not a businessman."

But Baako had stopped listening. She thought it was deliberate, the way he was staring past her head at the sky, yet his face itself had grown altogether expressionless, and the only feeling he showed came to her through his hands; he was holding hers, pressing them with a desperate intensity.

Over the wall the murmur from the cathedral swelled into a sung phrase that sounded at that distance like one inexorably rising cry, first of pure, impossible longing, then the fearful pain of impending disappointment understood, open sounds of hope still continuing in the face of every despair, and a long note of calm at the end. The words in her own memory.

> *Et exspecto*
> *resurrectionem mortuorum*
> *et vitam venturi saeculi*

Aaaaaaaaaamen.

Baako and Ocran were both quiet. A nurse came not long after the singing ended across the road and said visiting time was over for the morning. Juana did not feel like staying longer. She kissed Baako, and watched as he shook hands with Ocran, then she went out of the Asylum with the older man.

"I'm happy you came again," she said.

"I think I upset him," Ocran said.

"I don't know. He knows you're a friend."

"I hope so."

"I couldn't have said anything like that, straight, to him," she said. "I've wanted to, but it's hard. I've never had the guts to believe in myself, fully." She saw him smile. "He calls me a Catholic pagan on account of that."

"Yes, he should know," Ocran said. "It's the old missionary spirit."

"It should be something better, don't you think?" She'd tried to keep the sharpness down, but it was there in her voice. "Salvation is such an empty thing when you're alone."

Ocran laughed. "You don't find it in the marketplace. You have to be alone to find out what's in you. Afterwards . . ."

He didn't continue. He just shrugged, took her by the shoulders and drew her to him in a sideways hug then walked down the side of the road to his car.

A heaviness had come over her on her way home. Inside, she sat a long time trying to think, but her mind remained blank except for a continuing gratitude she was feeling for Ocran's presence this day and occasional, disturbing traces of the frustration she'd felt before. Walking around the house, she saw only lifeless things, till the idea came to her that she should begin preparing the unused room.

13 : Naana

THE TIME has come. What lies outside me is ready for me, and I too am ready to go. Such inward readiness to go does not come if this world here has room and use for us. When there is no use the spirit in us yearns for the world of other spirits, travelers who have crossed over from this side, just as the spirits themselves hope and wait for the new one coming. Here I have become the remnant of something that passed by and was immediately forgotten; the fruits that fell from my own entrails are looking hard for ways to push me into the earth deeper than where my navel is buried and to stamp the ground above me smooth with their hasty soles. And I have forgotten how to speak to them of the shame with which they have filled the last of my days, and of the sourness.

From the world and the life around me, nothing comes to me. My eyes are no longer windows through the wall of my flesh but a part of this blinding skin itself. Soon my ears too will be shut, and my soul within my body will be closed up, completely alone.

It makes me happy that inside me, in my spirit and in my mind, things have turned so that I can think I will soon be going, and think it with neither sorrow nor a single teardrop of regret.

How should tears come? What would I be regretting then? In the decline of my life I have found it hard to take out anything that has found its way into my spirit and to say of it that it has brought with it peace and the good stillness which understanding brings.

I have lived too long. The elders I knew and those who came traveling with me, they are all on the other side, and I myself am lost here, a stranger unable to find a home in a town of strangers so huge it has finished sending me helpless the long way back to all the ignorance of childhood. What have I to wait for, a traveler lingering in a wayside place where new things enter uncalled for and break into thirty separate bits the peace of my mind? The air here carries to my ears sounds that have no understood meaning, always with the loud and hasty wildness that is everywhere now. Since so much of what remains to be seen brings fear and the sights of day are followed in the night by this silent danger which has no name, I find it a matter in which the path of my soul has been good: that my body should be closing all the holes through which the world has entered me. In the end there will not be too many left to close with dust of gold, if I can think I have people behind me who will not begrudge me that final closing. There too is something to make me stop long and doubt, but this is not the time when I will eat away my entrails with thinking over things like this.

My spirit is straining for another beginning in a place where there will be new eyes and where the farewells that will remain unsaid here will turn to a glad welcome and my ghost will find the beginning that will be known here as my end.

Often the shadows into which the children of my womanhood have grown have seemed themselves to be groping blindly here, knowing no more than I who the other shadows in their paths may be. So even though my need has many times brought the thought to me, I have judged it useless to try and make them see my blind suffering and to cry to them for help. The cry has remained unmade in my throat, for outside there was nothing to receive it and turn it into balm.

It is so vague, the way I think I see them sometimes; and they, I know, see me as nothing at all. The larger meaning which lent sense to every small thing and every momentary happening years and years ago has shattered into a thousand and thirty useless pieces. Things have passed which I have never seen whole, only broken and twisted against themselves. What remains of my days will be filled with more broken things. Had I not given up trying to understand, to gather all this confusion together in my spirit and to see which way it was going, my blindness would have been insufficient pain for me, and to it I would have added my own madness.

Do I not remember how like a captured beast I was when I had not understood that I could understand no more? Like a small animal only freshly fallen in its trap, I was helpless while my eyes, my ears, my mouth, every opening in my body, took in each small sight and insignificant sound and searched it for its meaning. When understanding did not come immediately it only meant to me that the particular meaning of the particular moment was hidden some depth beneath the surface of the thing or the sound itself that had brought disturbance with it. So I looked more madly for what I could not find. But then every cracked bit of a moment some other mystery traveling past caught my eye, my ear, and the trouble of the time before was made deeper, not replaced, by a worse confusion. My spirit ran with a haste not chosen by itself, making of itself a joining path between too many things forever changing shape and size and color and above all unfixed in their meaning — rushing like an antelope near the end of its hunting, speeding this way and the other and almost caught again before it could come to rest and flung back with heart-burning speed always in search of a refuge it could not reach; until my soul screamed its terrible tiredness, gave up the rushing, unending journey and at last found rest in despair, not trying again to regain the larger meaning and the peace that can come from the great understanding. The world has hurried past me; I have grown willing to let it go, and I have not cared and suffered as much, till I am ready myself to go beyond.

All reluctance has left me. It used to bring such a sharp pain, the remembrance of young ones who in my youth died like single flowers in the immense surrounding green that shone too unwisely soon and too hastily alone, were noticed by eyes dulled with the unending green and plucked by hands knowing beauty only to grasp it with the force of their consuming hunger and to crush it with the death-giving fierceness they thought was love until the flower died from what it had called upon itself. I asked how it was known who was a witch and who was not, once when another strange woman was destroyed. I was told these things were known by eyes that shone too brightly in the day, and that a witch was a thing glowing with its own fire against the darkness and the peace of the night. I thought of witches growing in the peaceful green and flowers glowing in the cool darkness of nights till I fell asleep with thinking and seeing. My eyes are dead. Only the inward way is open to my soul looking to find its home.

There were even recently a few things remaining that had the power to bring into my mouth the taste of regret when I thought of this going that is coming upon me. One of these hopes has risen high and been brought down against sharp pebbles below, and if there is anything that will come after it, I fear it will only be a worse destruction.

The return of this one traveler had held out so much of good hope. But there were those left behind who had their dreams and put them on the shoulders of the traveler returned, heavy dreams and hopes filled with the mass of things here and of this time. And another spirit has already found its death in the hot wet embrace of people who have forgotten that fruit is not a gathered gift of the instant but seed hidden in the earth and tended and waited for and allowed to grow — so busy have they become in their reaching after new things and newer ways to consume them. Great Friend, I understand no more. I am coming where there is understanding to give a tired spirit rest.

If I thought I could still understand, I would be saying that I know the seed and the growing root of the restlessness that possessed the returned traveler and brought the others to shouting madness upon his head. He has been so quiet; and when in his presence, I have often felt a readiness to go away, a readiness like mine. But perhaps it is only that I have begun this thing the old ones spoke about: the habit those about to travel have of seeing a like readiness to go in all else around themselves. When I go I will protect him if I can, and if my strength is not enough I will seek out stronger spirits and speak to their souls of his need of them.

And the child that came so briefly has gone back where he came from: driven away, but who will hear me tell this truth? The child was thrown out into the world in haste, like forced seed. He was not pulled back underground by jealous mother spirits; that is only what Efua and her daughter Araba have been saying to hide their crime, after they have smothered another human soul in all their heavy dreams of things. There was so much haste to bring him out, and such a terrible loudness — the breaking of full and empty bottles and the swearing of unmeant oaths, the laughing of false laughter, strange quarrels and whisperings and the foolish pride surrounding the bringing out of each new gift, and that new confusing turbulence of wind turned on inside the house that day. I was powerless before the knowledge that I had come upon strangers worshiping something new and powerful beyond my understanding, which had made all the old wisdom small in people's minds, and twisted all things natural to the service of some newly created god. They have lost all belief in the wisdom of those gone before, but what new power has made them forget that a child too soon exposed is bound to die? What is the fool's name, and what the name of the animal that does not know that? The baby was a sacrifice they killed, to satisfy perhaps a new god they have found much like the one that began the same long destruction of our people when the elders first — may their souls never find forgiveness on this head — split their own seed and raised half against half, part selling part to hardeyed buyers from beyond the horizon, breaking, buying, selling, gaining, spending till the last of our men sells the last woman to any passing white buyer and himself waits to be destroyed by this great haste to consume things we have taken no care nor trouble to produce.

The little one is gone; soon he will be the elder of his great-grandmother there. The returned traveler also — in all that noise I thought he would surely die, but there must be strong spirits looking after him. Happy event if in his future there is yet something hidden that will reveal itself with time, though that will be long after I am dead. I do not know where he is, and they will tell me nothing. I know no way of reaching him and letting him know as I go that my spirit has been filled with thoughts of his happiness, that I have wished for him a life of good things done and a great peace at the end.

Nananom, I am coming. Long and often I have thought of this decline into you. Days when I was sick in my body or sick at heart or in my soul, I have reproached you for not calling me when I needed to hear from you. Nights when I was in the grip of some torturing disease and was wishing for the end of this long crossing, that I would be free of this wasted body which gives me no more pleasure, only pain — such nights I have dreamed of you and seen you in my dim sight clearer than I see anything in the world these days. My ears have strained after the sound of your voices, which have sounded in my soul like everything I have known: sometimes soft as the movement of leaves in winds bringing rain, sometimes quiet like rainwater dripping down tall, lean trunks of forest trees from the mat of leaves above to reach the soft soundless leaf-covered earth below, sometimes rushing and breathless like a young river, but most often a huge fantastic quiet like everything seen at once — the forests all the way to the horizon, the huge bowl of the sky waiting for the coming of the moon, deep, with no ending, silent. I have thought of you.

I did not know how easy the coming would be. I have been with you in dreams and night wishes, but often this was only when the world was not going well with me. Aches and fears and troubles brought my thoughts running to you.

I am confessing to you now. Be kind to me: a new child coming back to you. You knew me ready to die again and enter this world those here above think so real, this world which you know is only the passing flesh of everything that lasts, the soul of our people.

Coming home to you put fear into me at times. Do not laugh at me. I did not see you clearly, and I had been so long in this other world that I had no idea but fear.

Death. That was the frightening thing, the final sound. Now I see in it another birth, just as among you the birth of an infant here is mourned as the traveling of another spirit. Do not judge me harshly for the times I thought less of you than of the thousand things I had gathered around my body to give it comfort; they were to me then like living babies bound to me by thirty navels, and I thought I could never bear to cut them; there have been times when life was so sweet. For what purpose do you throw us such blinding sweetness when our aim is death?

I am reproaching you. Forgive me. I know of the screens of life you have left us: veils that rise in front of us, cutting into easy pieces eternity and the circle of the world, so that until we have grown tall enough to look behind the next veil we think the whole world and the whole of life is the little we are allowed to see, and this little we clutch at with such desperation. What a thing for you to laugh at, when we grow just tall enough and, still clutching the useless shreds of a world worn out, we peep behind the veil just passed and find in wonder a more fantastic world, making us fools in our own eyes to have believed that the old paltriness was all. But again we hold fast to the new shadows we find. We are fooled again, and once more taste the sharp unpleasantness of surprise, though we thought we had grown wise.

I am here against the last of my veils. Take me. I am ready. You are the end. The beginning. You who have no end. I am coming.